LIFE AND LANGUAGE
IN
THE OLD TESTAMENT

MARY ELLEN CHASE

LIFE AND LANGUAGE
IN
THE OLD TESTAMENT

GRAMERCY PUBLISHING COMPANY • NEW YORK

TO

MY MOTHER

EDITH LORD CHASE

who knew and loved the Old Testament

*This edition published by Gramercy Publishing Company,
a division of Crown Publishers, Inc.
by arrangement with W. W. Norton & Company, Inc.*

Contents

Foreword

THIS BOOK is a sequel or, perhaps more truly, an addition to *The Bible and the Common Reader*, which was published in 1944 and appeared in a revised edition in 1952. In that book I attempted to define the Bible as a whole, to give some knowledge of the history of the Hebrew people from whence it came, and to present its various literary forms, both in prose and in poetry, in such a way that readers might approach the Old and the New Testaments alike with greater intelligence and gain from each new understanding and enjoyment. The generous and widespread reception accorded it has now encouraged me to write this second book about the Bible, it to be confined solely to the Old Testament. Like my earlier book, this one also makes no claim to profound learning, but is rather the result of many years of reading and study; and, also like the first, it is intended neither for scholars nor theologians, but, instead, for the common, or general reader.

To read the Old Testament profitably and well is not easy. It presents far more difficulties than does the New. First, it is a much longer work with a far wider range of material, material which includes all manner of literary types from history, biography, and narrative to philosophy, prophecy, fiction, and many forms of poetry. Just as its content is wide and varied in scope, so is the life which that content portrays or suggests. Whereas the New Testament covers a period of less than a hundred years, the Old Testament embraces a thousand years in actual composition and many· more in subject matter. It is, moreover, as an artistic achievement vastly superior to the New, and because of that very fact demands more perception and discrimination on the part of its readers. Not only is it comprised of many differing literary forms, but it employs as many differing literary devices of which the reader must be aware. In order to discover within its prose and poetry even a portion of the treasures which each contains in such abundance, one must become familiar with the people whose work it is, with their singular type of mind, their ideas, and, above all, with their incomparable imagination which gave significance and meaning both to their thinking and to their literature. One must also know something of their land, responsible for many of their ways and words and for much of their outlook on life. And, finally, the thoughtful reader of the Old Testament must understand the unusual conception of history which unifies it; its idea of time so different in all respects from our own; and its various and unsurpassed uses of language.

This book, then, has to do, first, with the mind of an ancient, Oriental people, who have given immeasurable gifts to our Western civilization, and primarily with that creative and magical power of the mind which we call imagination. And, secondly, it concerns itself with the outward and visible signs of that imagination as they are revealed in the language and the literature of the Old Testament.

I would not for a moment suggest, of course, that numberless readers of the Old Testament are unfamiliar with its stories, known from childhood, with dozens of favorite psalms, and with many of the most beautiful passages in the prophetic writings and in the book of Job. Nevertheless, I have become convinced by many years of teaching its literature to college students and to older groups as well that few readers possess the necessary knowledge to discover the manifold gifts which even a single psalm may conceal beneath and within its outward form. What I shall try to do in the pages which follow is to supply some of the keys which will open the doors to a vast and rich treasurehouse of language and of life.

Mary Ellen Chase

SMITH COLLEGE

NORTHAMPTON, MASSACHUSETTS

A Note on Translation

A WORD must be said here about translations of the Old Testament since the overwhelming majority of us must read it, not in its original Hebrew, but in our own language. I am myself convinced beyond the shadow of a doubt that the one translation closest in the *tone* and the *spirit* of its language to its Great Original is the King James, or Authorized Version of 1611. I shall, therefore, cite all my references to that Version and make all quotations from it.

The several so-called Revised Versions, notably those of 1885, 1901, and the most recent Revised Standard Version of 1953, are indispensable to the scholar, intent on exactness and precision rather than on literary excellence; yet in every case their language is not only inferior *as* language to that of the King James, but fails to preserve, especially in Old Testament poetry, the beautiful diction, rhythm, and accent of that familiar and unsurpassed translation. Were these things not true, as they indubitably are, one might, indeed, urge readers to use only the King James Version on the grounds of greater familiarity alone. For more than three centuries it has been known and loved by millions and has influenced the language, literature, and life of all English-speaking peoples as no other book has ever done or probably ever will do. Yet my recommendation of its exclusive use by the readers of my book arises primarily from the honest conviction that as a work of literary art it is far superior to any other version.

In my own study of the Old Testament I have made helpful use of the standard Jewish translation called *The Holy*

Scriptures and published in 1917 by the Jewish Publication Society of America. This version, prepared by eminent Hebrew scholars, is of great interest and value to all readers of the Old Testament, Jewish and non-Jewish alike, since it is the work of men steeped in their own tradition and learned in their own ancient language. It is especially pleasing to note that in their Preface they speak of "the Authorized Version with its admirable diction which can never be surpassed," and even more pleasing to discover that countless passages in their own translation are identical with those of the King James Version.

If there are, perchance, readers who wish further and more conclusive arguments for the sole use of the King James Version as the source and basis for this book and who are interested in its history as a translation, they may find those arguments and that history in Chapter II, Part I of *The Bible and the Common Reader.*

PART ONE

The Ancient Hebrew Mind

THE CHAPTERS which immediately follow will attempt to define as simply and as fully as possible the Hebrew mind, those distinctive and peculiar habits of thought which marked the ancient Hebrews as a people, which, indeed, set them apart from other nations and races of their time. For the Old Testament, their one great literary monument, is the product of that mind and cannot be understood without the recognition of its essential and intrinsic qualities.

Throughout the Old Testament the individuality, the tenacious identity, of its people is again and again cited by its writers. They are chosen by God, to be sure, as His people; but clearly the choice has been made because of their own particular and especial attributes which make it possible for them, as for no other race, to fulfill His unyielding commands. In the 23rd chapter of the book of Numbers the ancient seer, Balaam, is made aware of the singular character of these Children of Israel. Urged by Balak, the king of Moab, to curse them as enemies, Balaam refuses. He can only bless them for, as he says, "they shall dwell alone and shall not be reckoned among the nations." In the 7th, 14th, and 33rd chapters of Deuteronomy, to cite but three instances among many of that book alone, they are defined as a *peculiar* and a *special* people (the Jewish translation in place of these adjectives says *God's own treasure out of all peoples*) and as one who shall dwell in safety alone. This somewhat ironic prophecy of safety was surely not fulfilled in the course of their tumultuous history; but their solitude in the sense of their marked difference from other races was always evident. Throughout their slow conquest of their Promised Land and years of uneasy peace, through exile in Babylonia and their return home, through their bitter existence for centuries as a subject people, they remained inherently the same, set apart by their inflexible and enduring identity. And even today in their new State, Eretz Yisrael (literally, the Land of Israel), they reveal their timeless traits in their consuming loyalty to tradition, in their active memory of their long history, and in their revival of their ancient language and insistence upon its daily use.

What, then, was this manner of mind, this inner life, which they possessed and which they recorded centuries ago in their *Holy Scriptures*, our Old Testament?

1
Its Background, the Land
of Canaan

NO SINGLE aspect or feature in the life of the Hebrew people contributed more powerfully to the making of their distinctive mind and imagination than did the land in which they lived. Not only did it dictate their ways of life and their means of livelihood, but it was to a large extent responsible for their thoughts, their zeal, their physical hardihood, their consuming loves and hatreds.

Before describing this land in its essential features, I should like to make more clear the name which I am using for it. The country of the ancient Hebrews is often known as Palestine, but this name was not known to them. It is derived from the word Philistine, or Philistia, and is of comparatively recent origin, dating only from the Christian period. The Land of Israel is a much more accurate name since it defines the country in terms of its people, who called themselves Israelites; but it is confusing because of the Kingdom of Israel, the name given to the northern division of the country as distinct from the southern, the Kingdom of Judah. I am, therefore, with some reluctance, using the word

Canaan, the name familiar to the Hebrew tribes when they conquered the land and made it their home, probably a century or so after their exodus from Egypt.

This Land of Canaan was a small land. From north to south, "from Dan to Beersheba," was about one hundred and fifty miles. From its eastern hills and deserts to the Mediterranean which formed its western border it was but some eighty miles in width at its widest. Its smallness alone, together with its natural barriers of sea and mountains, suggested aloofness and might even have defined security had not both been threatened by marauding tribes to the east and south, the Amalekites, Ishmaelites, Midianites, and others, those "children of the east like grasshoppers for multitude"; by the Syrians to the north; by the great predatory empires, Egypt, Assyria, and Babylonia, who for centuries had seen that narrow strip of land as a highway of trade; and for many years by the Philistines on the narrow coastal plain.

It was also a various land, one of extremes in climate and in crops. Although an overwhelming number of passages in the Old Testament refer to the *desert* and to the *wilderness*, to "a dry and thirsty land where no water is," and to the terrible east wind from the hot desert sands, which the prophets Hosea and Ezekiel describe as drying up the fruits and the fountains and which, the Psalmist says, breaks the ships, there were areas of fertility and plenty. Fruit trees flourished on the coastal plain, and wild flowers in abundance blossomed there, scarlet poppies, blue iris, and anemones, those Biblical "lilies of the field" which rivaled King Solomon in all his glory. Grapes grew upon the lower slopes of hills and mountains, and olive groves provided oil both for food and for religious usage.

In the north, in the kingdom known as Israel after the division of the country into two kingdoms, following the death of Solomon about 936 B.C., the land was far more open than in the southern kingdom of Judah. Here were wide valleys where wheat and barley grew; rich soil, which afforded prosperous farms like that of the churlish Nabal near Carmel, and vineyards like that of Naboth in Jezreel, coveted by the wicked Queen Jezebel for an herb-garden; water from the mountain streams of Carmel, Hermon, and Lebanon and from the sea-winds which brought more rain to this lower land than to the high, parched tableland of Judea. Here, too, were long roads where chariots like that of King Ahab could run, and over which Naaman, captain of the host of the king of Syria, could drive from Damascus to meet the prophet Elisha in Samaria and be healed of his leprosy in the river Jordan. It was the richness and plenty of these northern provinces of Samaria and Galilee to which the Old Testament writers repeatedly refer when they describe the mercies of God. They compare these mercies to the "excellency of Carmel" and to the fertile plain of Sharon; to plane trees by the riverside; and to the cedars of Lebanon, "full of sap," God's own trees which He himself has planted. They describe "a land of brooks of water, of fountains and depths that spring out of valleys and hills; a land of wheat and barley and vines and pomegranates; a land of olive trees of oil, and of honey."

Yet it was not the fair and open northern kingdom of Israel which bred the singleness and severity of the ancient Hebrew mind and character, but instead the austere, arid, and secluded southern kingdom of Judah, the land of Judea. Israel soon paid the penalty for her easier life; for her nearness to greedy alien nations; for her love of luxury and her tolerance of the infiltration of foreigners with the idols of their many strange gods. In 722 B.C. she was conquered by Assyria, and most of her native stock was dispersed and eventually lost. It was Judea who endured, who kept her kingdom for another century and a half and, even after her exile to Babylonia and return, preserved intact, even as a subject nation, her vigorous identity. It was this natural stronghold of Judea which was seemingly designed to produce in her people a sense of seclusion and austerity. Her prophets scorned the north for her traffic with foreigners; for her apostasy; for her dissolute indulgence in pleasure;

and for her treatment of the poor whom she has "sold for a pair of shoes." She has sown the wind, they say, and she must reap the whirlwind. It was Judea, not Israel, who was destined to give to the world the Old Testament.

This high, windswept land, physically the most barren, yet morally and spiritually the most fruitful region of Canaan, seems early to have been a lodestone, a magnet even to the patriarchs centuries before it was known as Judea, or as the kingdom of Judah. Abraham, the first of the patriarchs, whose name in Hebrew means *the lofty father of a people*, wandered into northern Canaan with his flocks and herds at some remote, undiscoverable time; but, if we can believe the ancient narrative, journeyed always toward the south country. Jacob, fleeing from Laban, his uncle, with his vast household and his asses, goats, and sheep, moved ever southward until he came to Bethel. And perhaps a thousand years later when legend gives place to history, David, who had ruled at Hebron for seven and a half years, was not content until he had wrested Jerusalem from the Jebusites and made its high hills his capital city, to become even from its beginning a sacred idea rather than merely a situation and a name.

It is easy to think that an inbred, natural love of barren and desert country made Judea a congenial home for the ancient Hebrews from Abraham to David. For they were originally a nomadic, shepherd people, wandering with their flocks over the eastern deserts long before they drifted into the Land of Canaan. They had known for centuries the violence of winds and sand-storms; withering heat by day and cold by night; the scarcity of water; the perils of hunger and thirst; the sheer physical strength and vitality necessary to wrest a livelihood from a forbidding land. The high, bare Judean pastures with their rough scrub and thorns, their white shelves of stone jutting out like the ribs of prehistoric creatures, their wide, transparent skies, were in no sense alien to them. They were, instead, another familiar home.

When the story-tellers, chroniclers, prophets, and poets

from 1000 B.C. onwards wrote, or gathered together from even older sources, the various books which make up the Old Testament, Judea, the origin of most of these, was a small kingdom or province, some fifty miles long from Bethel on its northern border to Beersheba in the south, and some thirty miles in width. Its central tableland, by far its most pronounced feature both in terms of area and character, rose two or three thousand feet above the Dead, or Salt, Sea. Toward this great inland water rocky and barren hills tumbled for fifteen miles eastward until they reached the lower Jordan Valley and the Sea itself. Among these hills, where roads were few and tortuous and where asses provided the chief means of travel, were countless caves like that of Adullam where David gathered his outlaws about him or like that of recent years, in which a Bedouin goatherd, in search of one of his straying animals, discovered the first of the ancient Dead Sea scrolls.

This wilderness of Judea, called in the Old Testament *Jeshimon*, or *devastation*, figures again and again in its narratives, prophecies, and poetry. Here David fled from the wrath of King Saul "upon the rocks of the wild goats"; here Amos in Tekoa, following his flock and gathering his sycomore fruit, brooded in solitude over the sins of Israel and God's certain retribution and punishment; here Jeremiah, a hundred years later, grieved over the sins of Judah as he looked down from his native village of Anathoth, only three miles from Jerusalem, upon other bare and broken shelves of rock. It was of such desolate hills that the Psalmist wrote, for among them were numberless valleys "of the shadow of death."

Yet even Judea was not totally a wilderness. After the rains there were green pastures and still waters for a time at least even in the most remote and barren places. There was the Vale of Eshcol, famous for its grapes; and there were villages like Bethlehem in the midst of fields and rich pastures. Here Jesse kept his flocks; and here Ruth, journeying from the Land of Moab, east of Judea, found labor and food upon the grain-fields of Boaz.

An environment such as this inevitably brought forth and nurtured a peculiar and a special people. Born to a loyalty toward ancient traditions and to a conception of their own history and destiny as both illimitable and solitary, they found in their Promised Land only more fuel for the fire within them which literally never died. Living, as their ancestors had done, always on the edge of danger whether from hostile tribes at home or on their borders; from wild animals or outlaws who, in the wilderness, threatened them and their flocks; from the spiritual peril of idolatrous neighbors who tempted them, sometimes successfully, with strange gods; from their harsh climate and the nature of their land itself, they became vigorous, alert, watchful, self-resourceful. The writers of the Old Testament are constantly calling upon their readers or hearers to *look, behold, hearken, wait, watch, listen, lift up their eyes*. It seems, indeed, as one reads its pages as though no one within them was ever unaware either of danger, or of difficulty, or even of the smallest details of the life about him.

Because of these very necessities there grew up also in the Hebrew mind a respect for the individual, his heroism, his initiative, his powers of endurance, his contribution to the common good, in short his *value*. This respect runs throughout the Old Testament. It is seen in the ancient story of Moses, who in Taberah after the Exodus, met by the criticism that two ordinary men have dared to prophesy as though they themselves were gifted with extraordinary powers, wished fervently that *all men* might prophesy. It is portrayed in Nathan's parable of the poor man whose one ewe lamb was stolen by his rich neighbor; and in the grief of Jeremiah over the carelessness of the individual soul toward God. Thus, in spite of violent revenge in times of peace and wholesale slaughter in times of war, behavior common to all primitive societies, there developed in the Hebrew mind an ethical sense unique among the nations of its day. This understanding of right and wrong, this ideal of justice to kinsman and to stranger, found its stern expression in their Law and rose to its highest manifestation in the condemnations and warnings of the prophets and in the ethical code of Job.

Their land, then, continued to nourish, to increase, and to intensify those mental and spiritual qualities which had early brought them as wanderers to it and which had resulted in their conquest of it as a people. The strength and vitality of their mind, its seemingly unquenchable and exhaustless powers of replenishment, never failed them. They could be conquered, but never really subdued; they could see their land laid waste by invading armies; they could endure famine, exile, persecution, punishment; but they always bounded up again if, indeed, they were ever really down! And this amazing fount of never-failing life owed its source in large part not only to the rigors of their background, but also to their conception of their history as a race and of their special and immutable destiny as the Children of God.

2
Its Conception of History

IN ORDER to read the Old Testament intelligently and well, we must always remember that it is marked throughout by the *historical* quality both of its thought and of its material. It is not only built around the history, the course of events in the life of a nation; it is in itself the social and spiritual history of a singular and distinctive people. This fact is made evident, first, in the so-called historical books from Genesis to First and Second Chronicles, inclusive, and in the book of Nehemiah, which together relate the legendary and actual occurrences in the life of the Hebrew race. It is made clearly evident also in the writings of the prophets and even of the poets.

The Hebrew prophets from Amos to Jeremiah believed and taught that God had revealed himself to His chosen people primarily by historical events; and they are always seeking to bring this truth home. Their interpretation of the life of their nation is, therefore, above all else an historical interpretation. When they *predict* the future, they see that future not in terms of some vision afforded to them, even although certain of them were granted visions, but instead as a necessary and inevitable consequence of past events or of present conditions. In other words, in their minds and teachings, the future of their race is entirely dependent upon the attitude, even upon the behavior, of their people toward the situations facing them at any given time. If they are careless and indifferent toward their responsibilities as individuals and as a nation, then their future must reflect the consequences of such an attitude and such behavior.

The Psalmists also write frequently of the relation of God to His people in terms of their history. Many psalms refer to the heroic figures of the past, to Moses, Aaron, Jacob, Joseph, Samuel, David. Several, such as the 78th, the 105th and 106th, recount as proof of the mercy and goodness of God the long history of the race as it is shown in definite and concrete happenings. The 136th psalm begins with the wonders of the Creation and continues with the bondage in Egypt, the Exodus, and the conquest of Canaan. Others, like the beautiful 137th psalm, describe a certain period or event, in its case the exile in Babylon. In short, history is ever present to the Hebrew mind, to its poets as well as to its prophets and chroniclers; and no understanding of that mind is possible without this recognition.

We must also remember always that history to the Hebrew mind was inseparable from religion. There was no history without religion, no religion apart from history. The two were one, an entity, indivisible. The active manifestation of the presence of God through historical events is not only at the very root of the ancient Hebrew religion; there is no religion without it.

This completely religious interpretation of history was unique and peculiar to the Hebrew nation. Nothing like it was known to other religions of the time, which were based, so far as we know, in no sense upon history, but rather, like most ancient religions, upon the physical processes of Nature, the principles of fertility and harvest, the ideas of death and resurrection derived from the familiar round of the seasons. Their gods were personified natural forces; and their various religious practices and rituals observed the succeeding cycles of the year. To the devout Hebrew mind all such religions and their usages were vain, empty, and idolatrous.

In their mind, had they made an image of their conception of history, or tried to picture it in any concrete, visual sense, that image or that picture would have been a long, straight, horizontal line. Even such a simple image, however, would have been impossible to construct and more impossible to conceive since it began at the Beginning and extended into a measureless and illimitable future. In that unimaginably far-off beginning God, the only God, who had existed before the making of the world, created the heaven and the earth out of darkness and chaos, made two great lights to rule the day and the night, set the stars in their courses. After His creation of man, who fell because of his insatiable desire to know Evil as well as Good, and after numberless other events lost in the abysses of time, their long line of history became marked or punctuated with the events known to them as the Acts of God toward His chosen people.

It was God, who had sent Abraham out of Ur of the Chaldees into the Land of Canaan; God, who led the descendants of Abraham, Isaac, and Jacob out of famine into the land of Egypt; God, who delivered them out of the oppression of Pharaoh by the hand of Moses; and God, who fed them on quails and manna and cared for them in the wilderness before they at last entered their Promised Land. Their Sacred Law, in its earliest traditions as well as in its final written form, was bequeathed to them by God himself. He went before them into battle against their enemies in the symbol of the Ark of the Tabernacle. He raised up their holy prophets to speak the words which He himself placed in their mouths. He punished His people for their sins both against Him and against their fellowmen, even against the stranger within their gates. He likewise rewarded them according to their righteous acts and their faith in Him. And although in their legends as recorded in the Old Testament there are many instances of His distinctly human and even inhuman behavior (primitive conceptions common to the childhood of all races) He was, in the highest conceptions from those of Moses onward, a God of Righteousness, Justice, and Mercy, who suffered for the sins of His children and who was always ready with forgiveness and recompense once they had turned again to Him.

The end of the long line, their *linear* conception of history, was, of course, out of sight. It moved always toward some far distant goal in some mysterious, undiscoverable future when all God's purposes for His people should at last have been fulfilled. Perhaps, indeed, no truer description of that line and its meaning can be given than in the exalted words of the poet of the 90th psalm: "Even from everlasting to everlasting thou art God."

God was, then, in the Hebrew mind, first and foremost the God of history, of human events and human experience from the beginning of life on earth, an active and even eager participant in the daily affairs of men, stern, demanding, and yet merciful. Only secondly was He the God of the cosmic universe with all its wonders. To be sure, He made Orion, Arcturus, and the Pleiades; the thunder and the lightning were His, and the bars and doors of the sea. He reserved the treasures of the snow against the time of battle and war; and when He laid the foundations of the earth, the morning stars sang together. These marvels are repeatedly attributed to Him, especially in the later books of the Old Testament and by its poets rather than its chroniclers. None of His manifold works is left unnoticed or unsung. Yet He is preeminently the Arbiter of human affairs, who is known by His true and righteous Judgments, whose Law is perfect, and whose pure Commandments enlighten the eyes of men.

Hence to the Hebrew mind as to no other, every event in their history, from its remotest beginning to its unforeseen end, held not only a profound religious significance, but was in itself a religious experience since it had been designed by God in His continuous and never-failing care for His people. And this God in the words of the Psalmist was the Lord, the High and Holy One, who has been their "dwelling place in all generations" and in whose sight "a thousand years are but as yesterday when it is past and as a watch in the night."

3
Its Idea of Time

I T IS almost impossible for the modern mind to conceive of a day undivided into hours and minutes. We are so accustomed to the ticking of clocks, to getting up, say, at seven and going to bed at ten, to making engagements and keeping appointments by some arbitrary and artificial figure on a dial, that we find it both baffling and mysterious to think of a time and a civilization which recognized no such divisions, felt neither need nor desire for any such neat apportionment of the days.

The Hebrew language had no word for *hour* and those who spoke and wrote it no idea whatever of such a period of time. The word even in our King James translation occurs only in the book of Daniel, a very late book in terms of composition and originally written at least partly in Aramaic, the vernacular of the day, rather than in the literary Hebrew of the rest of the Old Testament. This fact probably accounts for the usage of the word. In the New Testament, on the other hand, the word *hour* occurs frequently in the original Greek and was commonly used as that period of time under the influence of the Roman calendar. The only refer-

ence in the Old Testament to any time-telling device in our
sense occurs in the 20th chapter of II Kings and again, under
the same circumstances, in the 38th chapter of Isaiah where
the possession of a sun-dial is ascribed to King Ahaz; but the
word as translated is questioned by scholars and may mean
something quite different. If King Ahaz or his son, King
Hezekiah, of whom the story is told, perhaps under Assyrian
influence possessed some means of watching the lengthening
or the shortening of the shadow cast by the sun, we may be
quite certain that neither of them thought in terms of hours.

To the ancient Hebrews a thousand years might, indeed,
be as yesterday; or each of the six so-called days in which
God created the heavens and the earth might mean to them
an incalculable expanse of time. Nor must the events of their
history be understood as in any sense *dated* by them, placed
in any secure niches of time. These events are forever in
their consciousness, constantly in their hearts and before
their eyes, in their present as well as in their remote past. In
other words, the happenings of their history were timeless
to them just as were the incredible ages of the patriarchal
founders of their race, who are said to have lived any number of centuries from two to nine. One recalls Sarah, the
wife of Abraham, who at ninety years bore her son Isaac,
and Enoch, who lived three hundred and sixty-five years
and even then did not die at all in the natural sense. Perhaps
we can more easily grasp this vague, undeveloped Hebraic
attitude toward time, the complete unconsciousness of it in
our Western sense, if we compare it for a moment with our
innate habit of relating historical figures to definite periods
or even to exact years of birth and death. Nothing of this
was known or even dreamed of by the ancient Hebrews.

Their language itself as well as their use of it bears out this
fact. It possesses no definite, clearly-cut tenses like those
common to the Greek and Latin languages, to Western languages in general, and to our own. The two forms of Hebrew verbs, the perfect and the imperfect, distinguish only
between action which is completed and action which is still

going on. When one begins its difficult study, one is told that the best way to handle these verb forms is to translate the forms of the perfect as though they were past tenses and those of the imperfect as though they were future. But confusion inevitably results, for one soon discovers that the use of these so-called tenses is often inconsistent and that an action clearly in the past, at least from *our* point of view, is evidently still going on in the mind of the Hebrew writer. This is, in fact, the impression one receives even although one reads the Old Testament in English where the tenses are translated in accordance with our own sense of time: the impression, that is, that a seemingly completed action is never truly completed in the Hebrew mind and imagination, but still lives and moves in the present, and that those imperishable Realities which make his present will continue to make his future as well. In this sense his patriarchal ancestors have never died, and his prophets for him still live and will continue to live in his mind as they lived in the past.

This impression is increased by the curious and confusing disregard of chronology in many portions of the Old Testament where its writers are clearly either unaware or careless of discrepancies in time. An ancient poem of prophecy, written originally in the tenth century B.C., is placed in Genesis 49 in the mouth of the dying Jacob, who, if he existed as an individual at all, lived many centuries earlier. A beautiful fable concerning trees is spoken in Judges 9 by Jotham, the son of Gideon, although its actual composition must have taken place long before his story was written. Moses could not possibly have uttered his exalted song in Deuteronomy 32, for he lived many years before its time. The story of Daniel, composed about 165 B.C., arose out of the bitter struggles of the Jewish people under the persecution of the Syrian king, Antiochus Epiphanes. It was obviously written to lend courage and faith to those in revolt against him; yet it is set four centuries earlier in the Babylon of Nebuchadnezzar under quite different circumstances and, even within itself, contains most confusing chronology.

And, similarly, certain of the prophets are accorded a knowledge of events which took place hundreds of years after they had died.

What we have to try to understand is that when the ancient Hebrew writer told of events in the past, he did not remember them as we do in the light of the present, but instead took himself back into their time, real and living, if indefinite to him. Once securely back there, the things of which he wrote might well seem uncompleted to him. The present, merely *as* present, meant little to him since he lived in infinity. The time to which he was sensitive was not our time, governed by an inflexible, immovable, and absolute calendar. His time knew no perceptible beginning and end, no clearly defined past, no circumscribed present, and no discernible future except that in the Infinite Mind of God.

In place of hours, which meant nothing to him, the ancient Hebrew often lived and thought in terms of *seasons*, these not, of course, the natural seasons of the year, but, instead, some indefinite portions of time. He tarried for a *season* in some place; he remembered the *season* during which his people had come out of Egypt; he cried unto God in the night *season*. In the first chapter of Genesis God has seemingly himself determined this division of time, for He has placed the sun and the moon in the firmament of heaven "to divide the day from the night" and to be "for signs and for *seasons*, and for days and years." When the Hebrew writers refer to the only times of day recognized by them, they do so in terms of the natural divisions of *morning*, *noon*, and *evening*, times which, of course, varied in length depending upon the actual seasons of the year.

Some of the most simple, yet beautiful passages in the Old Testament narratives have to do with happenings and with familiar occupations at these natural times of the day:

> And Isaac went out to meditate in the field at the eventide; and he lifted up his eyes, and saw, and, behold, the camels were coming.

And he made his camels to kneel down without
the city by a well of water at the time of the evening,
even the time that women go out to draw water.

Nehemiah, returning from the court of Artaxerxes, king of
Persia, to rebuild the fallen gates and walls of Jerusalem, describes that restless work as "from the rising of the morning
until the stars appeared." God walks in the garden of Eden
"in the cool of the day." Ruth rose up from the feet of Boaz
at earliest dawn "before one could know another." Samuel
called Saul to the house-top "about the spring of the day."

Old Testament poetry likewise makes countless allusions
to these times of day. In the song accredited to David at the
time of his death, he describes the just ruler of men, who
rules always in the fear of God:

As the light of the morning when the sun riseth,
Even as a morning without cloud;
As the tender grass springing out of the earth
By clear shining after rain.

The Psalmist of the 55th psalm writes:

As for me, I will call upon God,
And the Lord shall save me.
Evening, morning, and at noon will I cry aloud,
And he shall hear my voice.

And the girl in the Song of Songs cries to her lover:

Tell me, O thou whom my soul lovest, where thou feedest?
Where thou makest thy flock to rest at noon?

In his Prelude to Joseph and His Brothers, the first of his
four novels on the story of Jacob and Joseph, Thomas Mann
gives a profound and illuminating description of the unfathomable past in the life of man; and although he nowhere
specifically defines this description as illustrative of the ancient Hebrew idea of time, that idea is surely present as we

may expect from his subject itself. Mann sees the illimitable past as a series of *time-coulisses*, or depths, the descent into which is impossible for the human mind and imagination. One is always halted, he says, in that descent by the impossibility of fully understanding even one's own beginning in terms of his remote ancestors. How, then, can he possibly retrace in these bottomless abysses of time the long rise of human civilization, its ancient traditions and legends eternally repeated in numberless races and tribes; its slow discovery of grain and equally slow domestication of animals; its creation of language, both oral and written? Mann's conclusion, then, is that there is no measurable time, since the past is lost in mystery and since all its depths and abysses belong not only to time which has gone, but also to time which is forever becoming. Therefore, all our past is in our present; all our present is our past as well.

No other portion of the Old Testament could lend itself so completely to Mann's treatment of time as does this primal, and primitive, Genesis epic or saga. Even the most literal of readers cannot fail to discover in that simple, pastoral narrative of wandering and wayfaring, of family relationships, of the time-worn tragedies, ironies, and even, comedies of an ancient, tribal people, the spirit of man forever moving on in search not only for the material needs of life, but for the immaterial. Yet one is not conscious of change here or mindful of the passage of time. Was this immemorial journey of Jacob and his household one of weeks, or months, or even years? Instead, what is intensely felt is an odd kind of permanence, not in the least at variance with constant, rhythmic movement, a permanence deeply rooted in the typical and the universal.

Willa Cather, in her comment on this first of Mann's Joseph books, has perfectly described both its effect on the reader and the identical effect of the ancient saga, its source. In so doing she has herself defined the Hebrew idea of time:

"This same dreamy indefiniteness, belonging to a people without any of the relentless mechanical gear which directs

every moment of modern life toward accuracy, this indefiniteness is one of the most effective elements of verity in this
great work. We are among a shepherd people; the story has
almost the movement of grazing sheep. The characters live
at that pace. Perhaps no one who has not lived among sheep
can realize the rightness of the rhythm. A shepherd people
is not driving toward anything. With them, truly . . . the
end is nothing, the road is all. In fact, the road and the end
are literally one."

4

Its Sense of Place

ONE OF the most distinctive features of the Old Testament, a feature sometimes disappointing to a reader
unfamiliar with it, is its lack of description, at least in our
sense of that word. The Hebrew language, in comparison
with other languages, possessed few adjectives, and even
these few are rarely used, especially in the Old Testament
narratives. Yet when they are used, they are meant to convey far more to the reader than he at first may understand.

The Hebrew mind felt intensely the *genius*, or the *spirit*,
of place. The outward aspects or details of any given place
may often seem disregarded; but the atmosphere which
these created or engendered, either through location, or
time of day, or association, was always of the deepest significance and meaning. A recognition of this fact is essential fo
one who would read the Old Testament well.

Place names are used in great number, but with them is
rarely any clear description of the place itself. Often, however, the Hebrew meaning of the name provides its own
description. Thus Carmel means a *garden;* Bashan, *rich soil;*
Bethshemesh, *the house of the sun;* Jeshímon, *waste and
desolation;* Bethlehem, *the house of bread;* and Bethel, *the
house of God.*

This deeply felt significance of a place, this awareness of its atmosphere, is admirably illustrated in the 28th chapter of Genesis, where Jacob, fleeing from the rage of Esau, "lighted upon a certain place and tarried there all night because the sun was set." Here he dreamed his dream of the ladder ascending from earth to heaven; and here God, standing above it, spoke His promises for the future of the Children of Israel. The Hebrew writer gives no description of the place except for the suggestion of darkness; but none is needed, for Jacob, upon awaking in that darkness, says: "Surely the Lord is in this place; and I knew it not. How dreadful is this place! This is none other but the house of God, and this is the gate of heaven."

Again, the same fundamental meaning and spirit of a place are brought acutely home when one reads of the death of Rachel in childbirth "in the way to Ephrath, which is Bethlehem." Her death, related briefly and even tersely in Genesis 35, is still fresh and sorrowful in the dying mind of Jacob when, in Genesis 48, he speaks his last words to his son and grandsons: "Rachel died by me in the land of Canaan, in the way, when there was but a little way to come unto Ephrath; and I buried her there in the way." Deborah, the old nurse of Rebekah, had died before Rachel on the same long journey from Padan-aram to Canaan. We are told only in the fewest words that she died in Bethel and was buried under an oak tree; but the brief statement takes upon itself new meaning when we learn that the name then given to the tree was Allon-bachuth, which means *the oak of weeping*.

A third illustration of this tone and spirit of a place, this atmosphere surrounding or within a setting, occurs in I Samuel 28 in the memorable story of King Saul in the house or cave of the Woman of Endor. Few details are given us, but we need no more. We see the floor of earth; the hopeless king stretched upon it; the smoky fire, and the meat and bread which the woman cooked upon it; her bed, upon which the king was finally persuaded to sit; the darkness of the night without, into which he at last "went away."

The prophets and the poets of the Old Testament are more generous with their adjectives and even graphic phrases than are the narrators; but even they are rarely lavish, and much given to repetition of the same descriptive terms. Their places are often merely *dark* or *dry, high, solitary,* or *holy, rough* and *crooked, goodly* and *pleasant, dreadful, thirsty,* or *desolate.* Yet these words clearly possessed for the Hebrew mind profound meanings; and the reader who is aware of this fact will not pass over them lightly.

There is a commonly used phrase having to do with place in the Old Testament, which should not be overlooked: *his place,* or often *his own place.* These simple and concise words are used in scores of instances. People are continually coming from or returning to their own places, their own houses, their own land, their own cities. Job's three useless and irritating friends come "every one from his own place"; the aged Barzillai, deaf and blind, refuses David's offer of a home in Jerusalem in reward for his loyalty and begs only that he may return to his land of Gilead and die "in mine own city." Even the Lord, the Holy One, is described in many passages as coming forth from *His place;* and one of the sages in Proverbs warns that a man who wanders from *his own place* is "as a bird that wandereth from her nest." In the constant reiteration of these words there is surely implied a sense of security, of possession, even of that identity characteristic of the Hebrew race and of the individuals who comprised it.

One immediately connects the security latent within these words with a longer phrase which also connotes the same sensitiveness toward one's own place, one's home, land, and people. We are told that in the days of Solomon every man dwelt safely "under his vine and under his fig tree"; and several of the prophets echo the chronicler by repeating the same words to suggest the same state of safety when wars shall have ceased, and men shall again be at home: "But they shall sit, every man under his vine and under his fig tree; and none shall make them afraid; for the mouth of the Lord of Hosts hath spoken it."

There is, then, far more than meets the eyes of the cursory reader in these bare and seemingly even barren references to places in the Old Testament. To the Hebrew narrator and poet the places which marked the history of his people or which formed the background for their fears, or hopes, or aspirations were neither bare nor barren. Secure in the knowledge that those deeply imbedded like himself in that history and that background needed neither interpretation nor detail, he used his simple and comparatively limited language not to describe what was already known, but rather to strike the always acute senses, to start the deep and abundant emotions of his race. It was not the outward and visible features of a place which concerned him, but, instead, its meaning, its spirit and genius, to those who had found it on their wanderings, or to whom it had been a refuge, or a curse, or an oasis of renewed faith and hope.

5
Its Distinctive Qualities

THUS FAR in my portrayal of the ancient Hebrew mind I have tried to present as clearly as possible its *attitudes* toward life in terms of ideas, its conception of history, its sense of time, its understanding of the spirit of place. I want now to try to show certain distinctive *qualities*, human and personal, physical and spiritual, which it possessed in such abundance and strength and which, together with its conceptions and ideas, marked its people as *peculiar*, *special*, and even *solitary* among the tribes, nations, and races of its day.

Long after the close of their legendary and patriarchal times, when the Hebrews entered upon the discoverable be-

ginnings of their history and had, after the Exodus from
Egypt, slowly conquered the Land of Canaan, they found
themselves in surroundings teeming with distractions and
temptations of every sort. The neighboring tribes, either
within their new borders or closely outside them, were
mostly of the Semitic race like themselves and doubtless
spoke virtually the same language. Yet their village ways of
life, their knowledge of agriculture, their employment of
metals and their use of tools, their stone houses in place of
tents, and above all, the various gods which they worshiped
with ceremonies abhorrent to the Hebrews, must have
seemed to these still half-nomadic Israelites not only baffling
and strange, but filled with dangers to their own strong sense
of national unity. The remarkable fact is, however, that in
spite of borrowing many new manners from their neighbors
and even falling from time to time under the influence of
their religious beliefs and practices, they were never ab-
sorbed by them, but remained exclusively themselves. Their
stubborn and critical wars with the Philistines on the coastal
plain, a people vastly superior to them in weapons and mili-
tary organization, wars which took place soon after their
conquest of Canaan, only served to weld their own tribes
and families more closely together as one people. David,
with that sagacity and shrewdness always characteristic of
the Hebrew mind, might make an alliance with Achish, king
of the Philistine city of Gath; but he was quite aware that
he was doing so only for his own temporary advantage. And
throughout their later history, whether they united with the
Phoenicians for their own interests or whether they were
forced to submit to the domination of great empires, they
never allowed their national individuality to die, but instead
maintained their identity to a degree perhaps unequaled in
the historical annals of any people.

This persistent, enduring, unconquerable tenacity with
which they adhered to and preserved their own ways of
thought, their own values, their own religion, had its pri-

mary source, one must believe, in their almost overwhelming vitality, both physical and spiritual. The very fibre of their race was vigorous and robust; and their natural hardihood, as has been said, was constantly increased through the demands made upon it by the character of the land in which they lived. The Old Testament is filled with people who possess this amazing strength and vitality, and obviously its authors love to depict them in these terms. Samson, we are told in his folk-tale, after killing a lion with his bare hands and slaying a thousand Philistines with the jawbone of an ass, picks up the doors of the city gates of Gaza, together with their two posts, and carries them on his shoulders forty miles to Hebron. Jacob wrestles all night with the angel of God. Jonathan with his armor-bearer crawls on his hands and feet up the precipitous rocks which form the Philistine stronghold and slaughters twenty of them "within half a furrow of an acre of land." Joab, the captain of David's army, captures Jerusalem from the Jebusites by climbing up the gutter on the steep face of the wall. Jehu, the son of Nimshi, "driveth furiously."

It is always amusing and yet significant to note that the Old Testament is filled also with people who *run*. They not only run, but, in the concrete Hebrew phrase, they "flee away on their feet." Abraham runs; Aaron and Moses run; Jacob and Laban run; Rebekah runs; David runs and leaps and dances; Saul and Jonathan are "swifter than eagles"; Ashahel, the young brother of Joab, is "light of foot as a wild roe." Nor, one must add, is this activity confined to people. Even God in the story of Joshua *chases* the enemies of Israel; the cedars of Lebanon *skip* like a calf, the mountains skip like rams, and the little hills like lambs.

The most restless and unwearied travelers in the Old Testament are Elijah and Elisha. The former is always appearing suddenly and without warning; the latter, according to the Shunamite woman, "passes by continually." If one takes the trouble to examine a map of the kingdoms of

Israel and Judah and to apply a scale of miles to it (for no distances in our sense of the word are ever recorded in the Old Testament), he will discover that the miles which these two early prophets cover are astounding. Whether they are going singly on their miraculous errands along the open northern roads of Samaria during the reign of King Ahab around 850 B.C., or wayfaring together from Gilgal to Bethel, from Bethel to Jericho, and thence to the Jordan, a mere matter of some forty or fifty miles, they are seemingly always in a hurry. As to Elijah, his one definitely recorded journey is perhaps the most astonishing event, at least in terms of physical hardihood, in the too few chapters given to him. In the 18th chapter of I Kings, one of the most striking narratives in the Old Testament, we are told that after Elijah had slain four hundred and fifty prophets of Baal in the brook Kishon, he ran ahead of King Ahab's chariot to Jezreel, a distance of forty miles. From Jezreel, to escape the fury of Queen Jezebel, he "went for his life" one hundred miles to Beersheba. From Beersheba, after a night's sleep under a juniper tree and two meals cooked by an angel, he continued two hundred miles to the wilderness of Mt. Horeb. It was quite fitting and proper that when Elijah came to die, he should be taken up into heaven by a whirlwind!

It is equally significant and also moving to note how frequently in Old Testament poetry the verb *walk* is used to describe not only a difficult act, but one often sur-. rounded by peril and despair. Did the poets mean to suggest that to run is easy, but that to walk requires all one's fortitude and strength? That to spend oneself utterly is less burdensome than to plod forever onward? That to "take the wings of the morning and dwell in the uttermost parts of the sea" is far less costly to the human spirit than to cause wells to spring up as one passes through the valleys of Baca, the valleys of sorrow? Job *walks* "through darkness"; the Psalmist *walks* "in the midst of trouble" as well as "through the valley of the shadow of death"; God giveth "spirit to them that *walk* upon the earth." Surely such a distinction in meaning is not only suggested, but clearly expressed in the beautiful verses at the close of Isaiah 40 with their impressive climax:

They that wait upon the Lord shall renew their strength.
They shall mount up with wings as eagles;
They shall run, and not be weary;
They shall walk, and not faint.

One is inclined, too, to cherish the notion that this native robustness and elasticity are reflected also in the lack of emphasis on illness in the Old Testament. If such a notion is the product of mere fancy, it is at least interesting and even amusing. At all events, to rescue it from the realm of pure conceit, far more learned Biblical authorities than I could ever claim to be have commented on the apparent healthfulness of the high Judean country and its wholesome physical effects upon its inhabitants. And, indeed, one is struck by the fact that people in the Old Testament who are ill from any cause are likely to dwell in Samaria or on the low coastal plain rather than in the hill country.

There is sickness, to be sure, but most of it is the consequence of sin against God's commands and, therefore, a punishment rather than the result of a physical condition. The Children of Israel are stricken with sickness because in disobedience and gluttony they eat too many quails in the wilderness; the presence of the Ark of God among the Philistines, who have stolen it from the hosts of Israel, causes a plague to curse them; the hated King Jehoram dies from a "disease in his bowels" as the punishment for his wickedness; and the child of David and Bathsheba is taken by God in retribution for their cruelty and treachery. The sufferings of Job are inflicted upon him by Satan, to whose power God consigns him because He wishes to prove to Satan Job's uprightness, even his perfection.

Little is recorded of natural illness, however, except in rare instances such as Naaman's leprosy and the sunstroke of the little boy of the Shunamite woman; and these stories are quite clearly told to prove the miraculous powers of the prophet Elisha. When people die, no discernible cause is usually given for their deaths except perhaps extreme old age. They merely die, or, in the case of kings, "sleep with their fathers." There is an almost amusing account of the boil which tormented King Hezekiah—clearly what we should call today a *poor patient!*—and which the prophet Isaiah cured with a poultice of figs. King Asa was diseased in his feet, probably from gout; but he presumably lived with it for some years as many have done since his day. And a famous heart specialist whom I know has been delighted to discover, with my modest assistance, that Nabal, the mean husband of Abigail, and Eli, the high priest of Shiloh, one of whom had eaten and drunk too much and the other of whom is described as *fat* and *heavy*, in all probability died of acute heart disease. The sick man in psalm 102 is as irritated and fretful as he is sick and apparently not a little resentful that, whereas God endures forever, his own days threaten to be "like a shadow that declineth."

In general, however, people in the Old Testament seem, at least, amazingly well. Health is rarely mentioned. Joseph does ask his brothers if the old man, their father, is well; Moses and Jethro, his father-in-law, exchange polite inquiries about the welfare of each; and Joab, before he slays his nephew, Amasa, with his sword, asks ironically about Amasa's state of health, so soon to be non-existent. And although the poets and the prophets write much of bitter mental and spiritual anguish, of sorrow, loneliness, and sin, seeing constantly, and truly, their country as a suffering nation from its physical dangers without and its spiritual perils within, neither they nor its narrators often record instances of bodily illness or even weakness.

Yet the Hebrew mind, always aloof and solitary, did know profound depths of loneliness and despair, more profound because of its very strength and vitality. This bitter distress is not only the subject of countless passages in the prophetic writings, in Job, and in the Psalms, where no loneliness of the human spirit is ever absent or unsung; it also lends its tragic note to many Old Testament narratives, some of these merely suggested by the bare and sparse words of their writers. There are few more lonely figures in any literature than Saul. Raised to a kingship which he did not want, cursed throughout his life, like Ajax and Hardy's mayor of Casterbridge, with the fatal flaw of jealous pride, loving unwisely and too much, he is a tragic, yet noble figure, bringing forth from us, like the Greek tragic heroes, only the emotions of pity and fear. Abraham, in the superb account in Genesis 22, knows the utmost depths of doubt and anguish possible to the human spirit when, alone on Mt. Moriah, he prepares to sacrifice his only son. Jeremiah in Jerusalem, homesick for the barren hills of his native Anathoth, recalling again and again the birds there which he loved, the partridge and stork, the eagle, crane, and swallow, says truly that he sits alone and solitary because of the unwelcome commands of God. Deprived, by these commands, of wife and children, even of entrance into the homes alike of those who make merry and those who mourn, he relates not only in words, but in the falling cadences of his style his complete loneliness. Isaiah, in the magnificent 6th chapter, which really begins his book, is aware even in his vision of God in the Temple that, because of that vision, he is set apart from the minds and thoughts of other men. The solitude of Job, sitting not only in actual dust and ashes, but in the dust and ashes of his traditional Faith, now revealed to him as false, knows no rivals in the realm of desolation and despair.

And what of the loneliness within those half-told or untold stories which tease the imagination of the sensitive reader of the Old Testament and of which one must never be unaware? In the 4th chapter of I Samuel there is such a half-told story of the nameless wife of Phinehas, the wicked son of Eli, a story only suggested, but perhaps more powerful for that very reason. We are left to construct it ourselves, to read what is unwritten of her hopelessness and sorrow. Dying in childbirth after the slaying of her husband by the Philistines, she refuses to look upon the face of her son, whom she names Ichabod after the *departed glory of Israel*. There are a dozen untold stories in the sad fate of Michal, the daughter of Saul and the first wife of David. Why was her loyalty to him so unjustly, even basely rewarded, not once, but three times? And what had been the haunting sin of the woman of Zarephath when she cries bitterly to Elijah: "What have I to do with thee, O thou man of God? Art thou come unto me to call my sin to remembrance and to slay my son?"

The Hebrew mind, as one might expect from its aloof and exclusive character, knew violence, too, and at times a truly fanatical hatred. Jacob curses the violence of Leah's sons against the men of Shechem; Leah storms in angry jealousy against Rachel, who, childless and desperate, has longed for Reuben's mandrakes, found by him in the field. Joab pays dearly for his violence as do Absalom and Ahithophel, and even David. In spite of his ruthless adherence to God's commands, few can forgive the violence of Samuel against Agag, king of the Amalekites, whom he "hewed to pieces before the Lord in Gilgal"; or his more bitter violence and hatred as a ghost, called up from his grave by the Woman of Endor only to curse Saul and to prophesy his tragic death.

The prophets, too, did not shrink from violence and hatred. Nahum's virulent poem on the destruction of "the bloody city" of Nineveh, "full of lies and robbery," pours forth revenge and fury both in its flaming imagery and in its unleashed, hurrying words. There is violence as well as scorn in the torrent of accusations hurled by Amos against the women of Samaria, those well-fed "kine of Bashan", who oppress the poor, crush the needy, and demand drink of their profligate husbands. Isaiah, his contemporary, is even more violent in his denunciations of the "daughters of

Zion" with their fine clothes, their earrings and nose jewels, their mirrors and crisping-pins. Instead of their perfumes, he cries, "there shall be stink" and "instead of well-set hair, baldness." Even the contemplative Jeremiah utters his violent curses both against the day of his own birth and against his backsliding, indifferent people: "Let their wives be bereaved of their children, and be widows. Let their men be put to death. Let their own men be slain by the sword in battle."

Such passionate outpourings foreshadow the violence of many of the psalms. For their poets hate as well as love; cry upon God for revenge as well as for mercy; curse as well as pray and praise. "Let his children be fatherless and his wife a widow. Let his children be continually vagabonds and beg. Let there be none to extend mercy unto him" . . . "O daughter of Babylon, happy shall he be that taketh and dasheth thy little ones against the stones!" Perhaps not a little of the ancient rancor and ferocity of their desert background survived through long centuries to break forth anew in these cursings. Yet without these occasional outbursts of violence the Psalms could never be what they together are: perhaps the most open revelation in any literature of the mind of a people in *all* its attributes. "I may truly name this book," John Calvin wrote, "the anatomy of all parts of the soul; for no one can feel a movement of the spirit which is not reflected in their mirror."

The honesty of the Psalmists, the truth, sincerity, and, above all, the thoroughness with which they reveal themselves, their baser as well as their nobler emotions, record more clearly than any other single portion of the Old Testament the universal, common heritage of man. They voice not only the aspirations and longings of all mankind, but the engulfing isolation and travail of the human spirit, far from God and unable to find Him. Characteristic though they are of the people from whom they come, they seem, nevertheless, to burst all boundaries of place and time, to become raceless and ageless. And in their veracity and candor, their utter lack of concealment or deceit, they complete in their poetry what had been for centuries the innate honesty and truth of the Hebrew narrators in their prose.

For the Hebrew mind was intrinsically realistic. That fact accounts for much of the directness and strength, simplicity and charm of the familiar Old Testament narratives. From the incomparable account of the tempestuous court of David, given in II Samuel 9 to 20 and I Kings 1 and 2 and originally written without doubt by some chronicler at that court, to the exciting tales dealing with the patriarchs, judges, and heroes but composed at a later date, there is no attempt on the part of their authors to conceal the most undesirable realities of human life and character. Not until later in its history did the Hebrew mind evince any power of sustained argument or of speculation, and even then to no marked degree; but from its earliest recorded beginnings it showed remarkable insight into the complexities of human psychology and of human drama. The lives and fortunes of individuals with which the Hebrew storytellers mainly deal are distinguished throughout by faithfulness and extreme candor. They record the vices as well as the virtues of their subjects and give the impression of detachment, on the one hand, and of intimacy, on the other. Patriarchs, judges, heroes, kings, queens, and princes, as well as lesser men and women are uncompromisingly portrayed. They are made to unfold and to reveal their thoughts, motives, and behavior, the prices paid for their follies, the inevitable consequences of their sorry mistakes and of their sins. None is idealized; few are ruthlessly condemned.

Jacob, known as Israel and given by God the responsibility for the making and continuance of the race, is as shrewd, cunning, self-seeking, and even cowardly as he is able, trustworthy, far-sighted, and intelligent. Joseph, with all his theatrical magnanimity toward his brothers in Egypt, is from beginning to end an irritating dreamer, an actor, a poseur, and an egotist. David, the founder of the Hebrew state and to future ages always the ideal king, is a bundle of contradictions, good and evil alike striving within him. He is merciful, brave, generous, naive, humble, capable of inspiring tenacious loyalty, kind to the unfortunate, and deeply religious; he is likewise ruthless, treacherous, cruel, sensual, subtle, and weak, a total failure as a father, a saint and a sinner, a master and a slave. In his brilliantly drawn portrait, remarkable among all biographies, ancient or modern, for its objectivity, its drama, economy, vividness and irony, not one of these conflicting traits of character is either disregarded or diminished. All are here.

Lesser characters, whether of the times of patriarchs, judges, or kings, are treated with the same straightforward realism: Hagar and her child in the wilderness of Beersheba, cast out by the jealous Sarah; Rahab, the resentful harlot of Jericho with her calculated revenge upon the men who have slighted her, and her scarlet thread; the left-handed Ehud and his secret errand "from God" to Eglon, king of Moab, in Eglon's summer parlor, especially built "for himself alone"; Hannah, the wife of Elkanah, who gives up the yearly family journey to Shiloh in order to enjoy her baby by herself away from the nagging Peninnah; Delilah and her wicked betrayal of Samson in the name of love; Jephthah, the Gileadite, his fatal chance to redeem his past and the bitter price which he paid for his rash vow. Even the more brief accounts of distinctly minor characters are often deeply moving because of the directness with which they are told: the stories of the ill-fated sons of Zeruiah; of Achan who coveted the Babylonish garment; of the dead Abner and his elegy; and of the mercy of Rizpah toward the seven dead sons of Saul, two of whom were her own. Each is etched sparingly, yet sharply, in an always memorable pattern. It is often, indeed, in these stories of quite ordinary men and women that the realism of the Hebrew narrator is at its best.

Yet all these attributes of the Hebrew mind, distinctive though they are and necessary to an understanding of it, are secondary to the emphasis placed throughout the Old Testament upon two other qualities even more character- istic: the sense of wonder and the instinct for worship. These are always recurring in narrative, prophecy, and po- etry, expressed either in words or implied in action and attitude. Indeed, without these two qualities the Old Testa- ment would lack its essential nature and distinction.

Wonder and worship are clearly most closely related, or, better, interrelated. Wonder, the sense of quick sur- prise, of astonishment, and of mystery, is in the impres- sionable and sensitive mind complemented and at length completed by reverence and worship. Worship, the eleva- tion of that mind to the Source of wonder, is thus insepara- ble from wonder itself. And both alike have their common origin in the mental powers of awareness, perception, and discernment.

In this inherent sense of wonder and this instinct and capacity for worship lay the rare and singular genius of the Hebrew mind—a mind seemingly lacking in those quali- ties which marked the intellectual endowments of other ancient peoples and which resulted in definite, tangible contributions to human civilization and culture. For when one reviews the more evident gifts and achievements of nations more or less contemporary with them, those of the Hebrews may seem in comparison meagre, ineffective, or even non-existent. They were not distinguished by mili- tary organization like the Assyrians, Babylonians, and Ro- mans. Their armies were always small and poorly equipped, nor did they have any desire for conquest except for the foreordained conquest of their Promised Land, or for war except that necessary for self-protection. They were not builders like the Egyptians, Greeks, and Romans. Solomon was the only ruler among them who seems to have en- couraged any extensive building program, and his proved unwise and eventually disastrous. Nor were they a seafaring people like the Greeks, or like the neighboring Phoenicians with whose "navies" they shared whatever trading by sea they entered upon. They were not skilled in the work of their hands and left no mighty monuments in stone and marble as did the Greek sculptors. Nor again like the Greeks were they philosophers in any speculative or theoretical sense. In fact, in contrast to other ancient nations they might seem a negative people; but this is precisely what they were not.

Although their peculiar genius was not bequeathed to future ages in any remarkable works of their hands or in philosophical conceptions and ideas, it was bequeathed in *words*, in that literary monument known as the Old Testament; and their rare gifts of literary expression owed more to their sense of wonder and their instinct for worship than to any other of their mental and spiritual endowments.

The ultimate source of both these qualities lay, of course, in their extraordinary vitality, both physical and spiritual. They were the most *alive* people of whom history bears record, alert, responsive, and forever watchful. Nothing escaped their eyes or ears; and everything which they saw or heard revealed itself to them in terms of association and meaning. That they were also great lovers was natural and inevitable. They loved life with passion, all its familiar earthly blessings, marriage, home, children, bread, animals, birds, trees, their mountains, hills, and waste places. And this devotion to life and its wonders was doubtless increased by the absence of any belief, until very late in their history, in any conscious existence after death.

As one would naturally expect, this sense of wonder has its most exalted expression in Hebrew poetry, in the utterances of the prophetic poets, in the Psalms, and in the book of Job. Yet it is by no means rare in prose, whether in the narratives of the Pentateuch and other historical books, or in the descriptions which the earlier prophets give of the circumstances under which they lived and worked. Nor is it here confined only to wonder over the sudden appearance of angelic messengers, or to the frequent miraculous tales which have their origin in legend or folklore, such as the flood, the Tower of Babel, the various plagues sent upon Pharaoh, or to the equally frequent relating of odd or ominous dreams, in all of which by their very nature we expect astonishment and surprise. It is likewise felt and expressed by many different sorts of people in the heightened moments of their own daily experiences.

In these ancient stories with their simple construction and their few realistic details this sense of wonder often sharpens and illuminates people, places, and circumstances. Abraham's servant is silent, *wondering*, as he watches Rebekah give water to his camels by the well; Jacob's words at Bethel are filled with awe and wonder; Joseph's brothers at the dinner which he gives to them look from one to another, *marveling;* the Queen of Sheba is so amazed at the wisdom of Solomon and all the glories of his court that there is no spirit left in her. The long chapters of the book of Exodus, told in a comparatively undistinguished way, would be dull, indeed, without the bush which burned with fire, yet was not consumed; the pillar of cloud by day and of fire by night; the thunderings and lightnings from Mt. Sinai; the sight of God, sitting on a great stone of sapphire, in clearness like the very heaven, which astonished the seventy elders of Israel. Deborah's famous song is sung not only in jubilation over the defeat of Sisera by the Hebrew tribes, but also in wonder that their strongest allies were the ancient river Kishon and the very stars in their courses. Gideon, that hard-headed strategist, the opportunist of the Old Testament, is overcome by an impulse to worship when he overhears the Midianite in the darkness tell his fellow about the cake of barley bread. Elijah on Mt. Horeb wraps his face in his mantle when he has once understood that the Lord has passed by, not in the wind, or the earthquake, or the fire, but in *a still, small voice*. Amos says simply that God *took* him as he followed his flock in the wilderness of Tekoa. Isaiah cries that he is a man of unclean lips before the sight of the seraphim and the sound of their *Holy, holy, holy is the Lord of Hosts.*

The reader of the 1st chapter of Genesis misses most of its charm unless he is aware of its childlike wonder latent in the simplicity of its words. It is as though the Creation itself were so incredible that any elaboration would dim the stupendous achievement. Nor is wonder absent from the mind of God. Through the account He is clearly astonished at what He is able to plan and perform: the two great lights which He set in the sky; the great whales which He placed in the sea; the birds "that may fly above the earth in the open firmament of heaven." Indeed, His own wonder is so vast, at least in the awed tone of the writer, that after each day He sees what He has done as *good*, and at the close of the sixth day, when He sees everything that He has made, as *very good.*

The perennial wonder and worship expressed throughout Old Testament poetry arise from various sources of amazement and awe. Perhaps the first and foremost of these sources is the never-failing mercy and goodness of God. The Hebrew poet exclaims repeatedly over His compassion and pity toward His own people through the course of their long history:

> *They wandered in the wilderness in a solitary way;*
> *They found no city to dwell in.*
> *Hungry and thirsty, their soul fainted in them.*
> *Then they cried unto the Lord in their trouble,*
> *And he delivered them out of their distresses.*
> *For he satisfieth the longing soul,*
> *And filleth the hungry soul with goodness,*
> *Such as sit in darkness and in the shadow of death.*

He exclaims, too, over the care of God toward *all* the children of men:

> *Let all the earth fear the Lord;*
> *Let all the inhabitants of the world stand in awe of him.*
> *The Lord looketh from heaven;*

He beholdeth all the sons of men.
From the place of his habitation
He looketh upon all the inhabitants of the earth.
He fashioneth their hearts alike;
He considereth all their works.

The glories and wonder of the physical world astound him, from the wise knowledge possessed by the fowls of the air and the beasts of the field to the snowy heights of Hermon, the clouds that shroud the Judean hills, the thunders of God which divide His flames of lightning. He writes with awe and even amusement of the hippopotamus, which moves his tail like a cedar and can drink up a river, even Jordan itself; of the sea-serpent, with which God plays as with a bird; of the strength of the horse, the glory of whose nostrils is terrible and who cries Ha! Ha! among the battle trumpets; of the goodly wings of the peacock; and of the hawk, who, by God's teaching, spreads her wings toward the south. Trees excite his wonder, the thorn trees and sycamores of the wilderness, the planes, palms, and cedars by the water's edge. Water itself forms countless of his images, more, indeed, than any other miracle of God's creation except mountains and hills, for in his parched and thirsty land it meant life and hope. He marvels, too, at the sea; but there is usually terror mingled with amazement over its vastness and mysterious depths, over its stormy winds and waves which cause sailors to reel and stagger to and fro like drunken men and be *at their wit's end*, or, in the original Hebrew, discover that *all their wisdom is swallowed up.*

In the 148th psalm these wonderful works of God are called upon to praise their Maker:

> *Praise the Lord from the earth,*
> *Ye dragons and all deeps,*
> *Fire and hail; snow and vapors,*
> *Stormy wind fulfilling his word.*
> *Mountains and all hills;*

Fruitful trees and all cedars;
Beasts and all cattle;
Creeping things and flying fowl,
Let them praise the name of the Lord:
For his name alone is excellent;
His glory is above the earth and heaven.

This persistent, unquenchable wonder rises even to ecstasy in the words of the poet of the latter part of the book of Isaiah when he inspires the exiles in Babylon to set forth without fear upon their long journey homeward across the desert. This poet wonders not only at the works of God, but over His power and willingness to adapt them to the needs of men. God shall lead His faithful people as a shepherd leads his flock. He shall carry the children in His arms and gently lead the women who are with young. To help them on their perilous way He shall also exalt the dry and parched valleys, make the mountains and hills low, the rough places plain, and the crooked paths straight. His people shall go forth with confidence and joy. Even the mountains and hills shall break into song before them, and all the trees of the field shall clap their hands:

The wilderness and the solitary place shall be glad for them;
And the desert shall rejoice and blossom as the rose.
It shall blossom abundantly
And rejoice even with joy and singing.
The glory of Lebanon shall be given unto it,
The excellency of Carmel and Sharon.
For in the wilderness shall waters break forth,
And streams in the desert.
And the parched ground shall become a pool,
And the thirsty land springs of water.
And a highway shall be there,
And it shall be called The Way of Holiness.
No lion shall be there,
Nor any ravenous beast shall go up thereon.
But the redeemed shall walk there;
And the ransomed of the Lord shall return,

*And come to Zion with songs and everlasting joy upon their
    heads.
They shall obtain joy and gladness,
And sorrow and sighing shall flee away.*

Several of the Psalmists are filled with wonder over the
very fact of human creation, over the gift of life itself. The
poet of the 139th psalm cannot sleep because of his realization that he is "fearfully and wonderfully made," that there
is not a word in his tongue unknown to God, or any of
his ways with which God is not acquainted. Such knowledge, he says, is too wonderful and high for his imagination to grasp:

> *Whither shall I go from thy spirit?
> And whither shall I flee from thy presence?
> If I ascend up into heaven, thou art there.
> If I make my bed in hell, behold, thou art there.
> If I take the wings of the morning
> And dwell in the uttermost parts of the sea,
> Even there shall thy hand lead me,
> And thy right hand shall hold me.*

Perhaps the idea of Wisdom is responsible for the deepest wonder of all. For to ponder on Wisdom arouses the
sense of mystery, a mystery profound and unfathomable.
Wisdom was from the Beginning. She was possessed by
God before He had made the earth, the mountains, fields,
and hills, the "fountains abounding with water." She was
then by Him as His daily delight. Her paths are unknown
to the fowls of the air, even to the keen eyes of the vulture.
She is a cedar in Lebanon; a cypress tree on the mountain
of Hermon; the Tree of Life to them that lay hold upon
her. And they that eat of her shall evermore be hungry:

> *But where shall wisdom be found?
> And where is the place of understanding?
> The depth saith, It is not in me,*

And the sea saith, It is not with me.
It cannot be gotten for gold,
Neither shall silver be weighed for the price thereof.
It cannot be valued with the gold of Ophir,
With the precious onyx or the sapphire.
The topaz of Ethiopia shall not equal it,
Neither shall it be valued with pure gold.
Whence then cometh wisdom?
And where is the place of understanding?
Seeing it is hid from the eyes of all living,
And kept close from the fowls of the air?
God understandeth the way thereof,
And he knoweth the place thereof,
For he looketh to the ends of the earth,
And he seeth under the whole heaven.

PART TWO

Imagination in the Old Testament

1

Conscience and Consciousness

IN THE fourth chapter of his book, *Culture and Anarchy*, a chapter called "Hebraism and Hellenism," Matthew Arnold discusses the two great sources, or streams of influence upon our Western civilization and culture in terms of their respective contributions, moral, ethical, aesthetic, and spiritual. He makes a sharp distinction between the two, that is, between the Hebraic and the Hellenic, the Hebrew and the Greek. Granting as he does that both the Hebrew and the Greek mind held as a common goal the slow progress of man toward ultimate perfection, he claims, nevertheless, that they pursued this lofty aim in two diametrically opposite ways. He asserts that the ancient Hebrews were governed by obedience to their Sacred Law and to the Will of God as expressed within it, in other words by *strictness of conscience*, whereas the Greeks were governed by *spontaneity of consciousness*. Or, to put it more simply, that the Hebrews saw life in terms of *conduct*, whereas the Greeks saw life in terms of *thought and beauty*; in short, that the Greeks saw things as they really *are*, but that the Hebrews, governed by the rules of behavior and action rather than by thought and perception, did not, indeed *could* not, see things as they really *are*. "Nothing," Arnold says, "can do away with this ineffaceable difference." Throughout his chapter he is implying, of course, that the Greek imagination, which was alike the source and the product of their spontaneity of consciousness, was in every sense more profound and far more rich than was the Hebrew imagination and could, therefore, contribute more to future ages, especially in the realm of aesthetic and spiritual values.

Of course, there is more than an element of truth in Arnold's chief contention: that the Hebrews saw life in terms of conduct, whereas the Greeks saw it in terms of thought and beauty. But the source and basis of this contention rests upon only *one* contribution of the ancient Hebrews: their insistence upon the Law of God, both in its recorded form and in the awareness of it through tradition and history centuries before it actually took shape in the hands of the priests, and upon its strict observance by an unquestioning adherence to all its rigid rules and restrictions. From this contribution, the greatness of which Arnold does not for a moment minimize, arises his conviction that to the Hebrew mind a man's behavior was of far greater importance than his ways of thought; that, indeed, the rules laid down for him often impoverished his power of thinking.

What, then, was this Sacred Law of the Hebrew people?

And why did Arnold see in it their chief contribution to the life and to the manner of thought of later civilizations? The answers to these questions are both important in themselves and pertinent to the subject of this book; for, as a matter of fact, this Law, or Covenant between God and His people, has had a great deal to do with blinding countless persons through many centuries to the real nature of the Hebrew genius. Arnold is by no means alone in his judgment concerning the vast and relentless power of this written and unwritten Law, its emphasis on *strictness of conscience* at the expense of *spontaneity of consciousness*, on *doing* at the cost of *being*. But since there are those, of whom I am one, who believe sincerely that he grossly underestimated the richness of the ancient Hebrew imagination, it is well to understand more fully the basis of his judgment.

The written Law of the Hebrew nation, their *Torah*, is contained in the Pentateuch, in the books of Deuteronomy and Leviticus, and in portions of Exodus and Numbers. Its core and center were the Ten Commandments, supposedly given by God from Mt. Sinai to Moses after he had led the Children of Israel out of bondage in Egypt, but actually written centuries later. Around these Commandments there grew up over a period of centuries a vast number of other laws having to do with civic and ethical as well as religious obligations, with a man's duty toward his nation, his society, his family, his neighbor, the stranger within his gates, but, above all, with his sacred duty toward his God. Together with these specific laws there were also many rules and restrictions which should control these obligations. And, in addition, there were almost numberless rites and ceremonies which were to be performed not only in the Temple at Jerusalem, but in synagogues and even in homes.

This, in a simple and most abbreviated definition, was the Hebrew Law. Originally recorded in the book of Deuteronomy, which was said to have been "discovered" in the Temple at Jerusalem in 621 B.C., it was greatly increased by the numerous laws recorded in Leviticus some two centuries later and by other laws which we find inserted elsewhere in the Pentateuch. Later these laws were assembled and codified by the priests and established as the Sacred Law of the Hebrew nation, to become, in the minds of both priests and people, the earthly constitution of the Kingdom of God.

When we read it today, if indeed we *can* read it, it seems not only meaningless, but so rigid and uncompromising, so exclusive with all its minute inclusiveness, as to be almost a document of enslavement. Yet we must never forget that to a small and subject nation, always, after the exile in Babylon in 586 B.C. and return to Jerusalem fifty years later, under the domination of foreign powers, it meant quite literally the survival of a people. Deprived of their rights of self-government and surrounded by alien influences which they hated and feared, they looked upon their Law as a sacred institution which alone could keep alive in their minds their traditions and their peculiar history as God's chosen people. Without its control they could not have continued their existence as a nation in the midst of a world always indifferent and often hostile toward their religious faith.

All of us are familiar with the statement that *the Law superseded the prophets*. What precisely does it mean? It means that, in the minds of the priests, always the scholars and the leaders of Hebrew thought, the teachings and the visions of the great prophets, Amos, Hosea, Isaiah, Micah, and Jeremiah, exalted though they were and woven into the very fabric of the dreams and aspirations of the Hebrew nation, were, nevertheless, too intangible and too visionary for any prescribed system of life, any daily practice of religion. The priests, who had in their charge the preservation of the national faith, were both conservative and extremely realistic men. They were ancient psychologists as well. Not only were they themselves committed to the establishment of what they believed to be the prescribed Law of God, but the administration of it was committed to their charge. They recognized, as many other religious teachers since their day have done, that to the mass of people a rule or a law, tangible and definite, is easier to understand and to follow than an idea or a principle, however lofty or inspired. They realized also that the application of such rules and laws may mean a unity of thought and action impossible without them; and that their strict observance often may result even in a better and more just human society.

And what of the great prophets whom this Law had *superseded?* Were they forgotten? Were their fervent utterances, which proclaimed God as the sole and universal God, which taught that "to do justly, and to love mercy, and to walk humbly" with Him is all that He requires of men, which condemned the sins of hypocrisy, idolatry, and social injustice, lost to the Hebrew nation? By no means. Their conceptions of God and of man's duty toward Him and toward all men, whom He made in His own image, were not only preserved in their own books, canonized as a portion of the Holy Scriptures by the priests and scholars who prepared the Old Testament, but many of their ideals for human conduct were incorporated within the Law itself.

In several chapters of the book of Deuteronomy, most of which is purported to be a sermon given by Moses, these ideals are evident in the eloquent words of its unknown writer, who clearly had been deeply influenced by prophetic teaching:

> And thou shalt love the Lord thy God with all thine heart and with all thy soul, and with all thy might. And these words, which I command thee this day, shall be in thine heart. And thou shalt teach them diligently unto thy children, and shalt talk of them

when thou sittest in thy house, and when thou walk-
est by the way, and when thou liest down, and when
thou risest up. And thou shalt bind them for a sign
upon thine hand, and they shall be as frontlets between thine eyes. And thou shalt write them upon
the posts of thy house and on thy gates.

For the Lord your God is God of gods, and Lord
of lords, a great God, a mighty and a terrible, which
regardeth not persons, nor taketh reward. He doth
execute the judgment of the fatherless and widow,
and loveth the stranger in giving him food and
raiment. Love ye therefore the stranger: for ye were
strangers in the land of Egypt.

Thou shalt not oppress an hired servant that is
poor and needy, whether he be of thy brethren or
of thy strangers that are in thy land within thy gates.

In Leviticus, which is almost entirely a succession of dreary
laws pertaining to food, sacrifices, holy days, and even to
the most minute details of human existence, one finds the
command usually attributed to Jesus, but in reality in the
ancient Hebrew Law:

Thou shalt love thy neighbor as thyself.

Nor must one forget that six of the Ten Commandments
have to do not with graven images, or with blasphemy, or
with the observance of the Sabbath, but instead with a man's
obligations to the society in which he lives and to his fellowmen.

Yet in fairness to Arnold's contention that the ancient
Hebrews saw life in terms of conduct, we must acknowl-
edge that the emphasis of prophetic teaching, whether incorporated within the Law or surviving in its own nobility
of thought and utterance, was primarily on human behavior, on God's requirement of every man to do justly,
and to love mercy, and to walk humbly with his God. The
prophets believed that they had been called by God to

reform the evil times upon which their nation had fallen and to save a sinful people from the sure and certain punishments of a righteous God. The language in which they spoke and the thoughts and aspirations which actuated it were a far cry from the rigidity of the great body of the Law; yet their teachings were mainly ethical and social even although always within them glowed the light of the spirit.

It was this primary emphasis on human conduct whatever its religious aspiration of which Arnold was thinking, of the rules laid down for it, of the punishments which were the inevitable consequences of their violation. He was recalling the mighty influences of such emphasis through the succeeding centuries: in the teachings of St. Paul, who never freed himself from the rigors of the old Law in which he had been trained, even though he preached a New Covenant, the major premise of which was that men are justified by Faith rather than by their works, however good; in the terrible rigidities of Puritanism, necessary as was its stern moral fibre to its times; in John Calvin's theocratic society in Geneva and its successor in the Scotland of John Knox. For although Calvin might and, indeed, did see in the Psalms "the mirror of the spirit" and "the anatomy of the soul," it was the *Thou shalt* and *Thou shalt not* of the Law which built his theocratic state. And not only the prescribed and recorded Law, but that which he discerned throughout the Old Testament, the emphasis on conscience and conduct, the rewards of righteousness, the punishments of evil, from Adam's fall and Reuben's sin to the wickedness of Belshazzar. To him and to all the Puritans who followed him the Old Testament was not even dimly the record of a thousand years of a people's tradition and history, their fears and hopes, their human longings, dreams, and visions. It was clearly the Word of God, the divine command, an unalterable rule of life.

The power which lay behind our Authorized, or King James Version was this same conviction, never absent from

the minds and consciences of its translators. They believed
that they were in reality putting into English words the
veritable Law and Word of God, given by His hand to
Moses at some definite and even discernible time. It was
this stern conviction which actuated their work. And although among the fifty-four, chosen from both Anglicans
and Puritans for the holy task, there must have been poets
as well as scholars—else how could they have achieved
such beauty and perfection of language?—their first and
most sacred duty was to make possible for the common man
a more accurate knowledge of God's Holy Word, the
Covenant which He had established for all time between
himself and all men. This invulnerable faith is clearly seen
in their words addressed to the Reader in the preface of their
Version:

> And what marvel? the original thereof being from
> heaven, and not from earth; the author being God,
> not man; the inditer, the Holy Spirit, not the wit of
> the Apostles or Prophets; the form, God's word,
> God's Testimony, God's oracles, the word of truth,
> the word of salvation.

It is one of the strange and unsolvable mysteries that the
Puritans, both in England, and in America in the seven-
teenth and eighteenth centuries, should seemingly have been
so blind to the unbound spirit of man, to its dreams, passions, and fancies, to its imaginative life, all of which, except for the books of the Law, illuminate the pages of the
Old Testament. Did they ignore or else consign to some
small, remote, well-guarded corner of their minds all the
hope and wonder of the Psalmists, all the boundless ecstasies of the prophetic poets, all the mystical nature of
Wisdom, all of Job's doubts and unanswered questions concerning the justice of God toward men? But perhaps the
mystery is less dark and unsolvable when we consider how
our own forefathers, not too far removed from us, themselves looked upon the Old Testament. To them, too, its

commands were more powerful than its promises, its rewards and punishments more memorable than the beauty of its language. Even in my own childhood, as perhaps in that of yours who are reading these words, the Bible, in our idea of it, told us what to *do* rather than what to *be* or to *become* within our innermost selves, how to escape the anger of God rather than how to sense His greatness, or the mystery of His Being, or the wonders of His works.

To this day there still clings about the Bible an aura of sacred piety, and not alone among those sects which continue to see it as the unalterable Word of God, literally "true" in every line and syllable. The most modern of readers hardly approaches it as he approaches the *Iliad* and the *Odyssey*, in large part doubtless contemporary with the Old Testament. We cannot quite free ourselves of the uncomfortable notion, or perhaps even comfortable, that the reading and the study of it are somehow connected with our lives in terms of our behavior, that we shall conceivably become *better* from a knowledge of it.

Perhaps, indeed, we shall be *better* for our reading of the Old Testament; but only if we are able to understand that adjective as Euripides understood it when he says to Aeschylus in the play of Aristophanes that a poet should be admired "because through his genius he makes men better in their cities." Or, if we are able to grasp the inner thought of the Psalmist when he cries that the word of God is "a lamp unto his feet and a light unto his path." Both Euripides in his definition of the poet and the Psalmist in his figures of light suggest that this *betterment* is of the mind and the spirit, that one truly lives only within their realm, that, indeed, all outside it is, in comparison, unreal and meaningless.

The power which created Euripides' understanding and the Psalmist's images was the power of the human imagination. That the ancient Greeks possessed that power in all its forms, no one who has read their literature or looked upon the surviving creations of their art has ever doubted. It will be my hopeful pleasure in the following chapters to prove that the ancient Hebrews possessed it likewise in equal, if not greater strength and richness, and that the peculiar power of their imaginative vision has given to the Old Testament, both in thought and in language, its enduring genius.

2

The Hebrew Imagination

SINCE this chapter is to be a portrayal, or perhaps even an analysis of the ancient Hebrew imagination, we cannot, I think, do better than to compare it with the imagination of the ancient Greeks as it is revealed in the *Iliad* and the *Odyssey*. These great epics were, as I have said, in large part contemporary with much of the Old Testament in terms of composition. Moreover, the slow creation of both was similar, each being the work of many hands through many centuries. The Greek epics and the Old Testament have alike wielded mighty influences upon our Western ways of life and thought. Indeed, from their respective methods of composition much of our own Western literature has sprung.

Arnold's statement, that the Greeks saw things as they really *are* but that the Hebrews did not, deserves some clarification before its truth can be seriously challenged. Just what does it mean to see things as they really *are?*

It means, first of all, to see things with keen and alert powers of observation, with complete comprehension, their shapes, lines, forms, lineaments, colors, all their outward and visible features and aspects. Thus the god Hermes sees the cave of Calypso on her island:

But when he had reached that far-off isle, he went forth from the sea of violet blue to get him up into the land till he came to a great cave. . . . And around about the cave there was a wood blossoming, alder and poplar and sweet-smelling cypress. And therein roosted birds, long of wing, owls, and falcons and chattering sea-crows, which have their business in the waters. And, lo, there about the hollow cave trailed a gadding garden vine, all rich with clusters. And fountains four, set orderly, were running with clear water, hard by one another, turned each to his own course. And all about soft meadows bloomed of violets and parsley.[1]

Thus Jacob sees as clearly, if with less detail, the well at Haran:

Then Jacob went on his journey and came into the land of the people of the east. And he looked and, behold, a well in the field, and, lo, there were three flocks of sheep lying by it, and a great stone was upon the well's mouth. And thither were all the flocks gathered.

But there are also qualities as well as outward aspects of things seen, characteristics which reveal their inner nature. To these also the imaginative mind is always awake. Both Homer and the poet of the Old Testament were keenly aware of the nature of the ass, the beast of burden to all ancient people and always intractable and stubborn. Homer compares the doggedness of the Trojan heroes in their fight against Ajax to the stubborn ass:

Even as an ass going beside a field overpowers the boys who drive him, a dull ass about whose back

[1] The quotations from the Greek epics, both in this chapter and the one following, are taken from Lang, Leaf, and Myers, *The Iliad*, and Butcher and Lang, *The Odyssey*. I have purposely chosen these translations since their language is similar in many ways to that of the Old Testament in the Authorized Version. In two cases the translations are from Gilbert Murray's *The Rise of the Greek Epic*.

many a staff is broken; and he enters the standing corn and ravages it, and the boys smite him with sticks. But their strength is feeble, and scarcely do they drive him out when he has had his fill of the corn.

The poet of the book of Job describes the nature of the wild ass, similar surely to his Hellenic brother:

> *He scorneth the multitude of the city,*
> *Neither regardeth he the crying of the driver.*
> *The range of the mountains is his pasture,*
> *And he searcheth after every green thing.*

Birds of various kinds fly constantly across the pages both of the Greek epics and the Old Testament. They are always described with acute observation of their nature and ways. Homer pictures the cranes:

> The screaming of cranes riseth in front of the sunrise, cranes that have fled from winter and measureless rain. Screaming, they fly over the streams of ocean.

He knows the cormorants, too:

> Then Hermes sped along the waves like the cormorant that chaseth the fishes through the perilous gulfs of the unharvested sea, and wetteth his thick plumage in the brine.

The prophets and poets of the Old Testament know that the wide wings of the stork hold the wind within them; that the mourning of those who are sad is as the mourning of the dove; that the eagle stirreth up her nest and fluttereth over her young, bearing them upon her wings. King Hezekiah complains in his illness that his teeth chatter with the sound of the swallow and the crane and that his moaning in his anguish is like the moaning of the dove. And the pilgrims of the 84th psalm as they near Jerusalem see with wonder that the birds are building their nests even among the stones of the Temple:

> Yea, the sparrow hath found a house,
> And the swallow a nest for herself
> Where she may lay her young.
> Even thine altars, O Lord of Hosts,
> My King, and my God.

We have already become acquainted with the intrinsic realism of the Hebrew mind, its veracity and candor shown in its portrayal of human character and in its delineation of all human emotions. It was this same realism which allowed nothing of outward form or of inward quality to escape the eyes and the perceptions of Hebrew writers. But, as we have seen, too, they possessed also in even greater measure than their realism, an innate sense of wonder and an instinct for reverence and worship. These two qualities extended their powers of imagination far beyond the outward appearance or even the inner quality of the objects which they described with such sensitive accuracy. Like the Greek writers they saw things with vividness and clarity, in other words, things as they outwardly and inwardly *are;* but, far more than the Greeks, they saw everything in terms of memory, the long, persistent, tenacious memory, not of an individual, but of a race.

This does not, *cannot,* of course, mean that the writer, or writers, of the great Greek epics did not also see things in terms of association. The beautiful Homeric similes which appear on a hundred pages of both the *Iliad* and the *Odyssey* to delight us with their brilliant imagery and their amazing detail, images of wind, snow, wasps, "high-crested oak trees," fire, mists, the waves of the wine-dark sea, disprove any such mad statement. The Greek epics without this rich associative power could never have endured through the ages as triumphs of the human imagination. Yet the careful reader of both Homer and the Old Testament

is again and again made aware that the associative power of
the Hebrew mind and of the writers who record it is not
only different in its nature and use from that of the Greek
mind as shown in the epics, but in certain ways more profound and more vast.

The reasons for this difference, if, indeed, the Hebrew
writers do show more profound and more vast powers of
association and, therefore, of imagination are, of course, of
the utmost importance. The first one lay in their respective
languages and in the use of each. The Greek in comparison
with the Hebrew was a highly sophisticated and elegant
language even in the days before its Golden Age of Pericles.
It lent itself to elaborations and embellishments of every
sort. It was flexible and fluent, melodious and liquid. It
could weave in and out of patterns as intricate as those of
Ariadne's labyrinth and yet never lose itself. It was rich
and beautiful with descriptive and compound words, the
rosy-fingered Dawn, the gray-eyed Athene, the silver-
bowed Apollo, Zeus, the cloud-gatherer, Poseidon, the
earth-girdler. Beside it, the language spoken and written by
the ancient Hebrews was rough and crude, scant, limited by
its lack of constructions, unmusical, even discordant in
sound. It was not made for ornament. Its images were sharp
and concrete, simple like the simple, unsophisticated, un-
traveled writers who used it. It came from a barren, bare,
and thirsty land, not from the blue islands of the Aegean,
or the rich land of the Lotus Eaters, or a country of "bright
waters and unfailing cisterns."

And yet its solitary, gaunt images and figures, seeming to
hold nothing beyond brief and often stark words, evoke an
association impossible to the detailed and lavish ones of
Homer.   *The shadow of a great rock in a weary land.*
*The waste and howling wilderness.   The stones of dark-
ness and the shadow of death.   A covert from storm
and from rain.   A land of darkness, as darkness itself.*

As each sprang from the limitless and profound imagination of its writer, always aware of the past of his race and land, so each in the mind of its reader arouses a train of associations largely because of its very loneliness and solitude. Homer tells us all in his minutely described images, his detailed and beautiful figures: how a little girl snatches at her mother's gown and, in tears, begs to be taken up; how women wash their clothes in the river and spread them to dry on the clean pebbles; how cows walk with "their trailing feet and shambling gait." We see them all through his marvellous power of imaginative creation, so marvelous, indeed, that there is little left for our own imaginative powers to create.

A second reason, and perhaps an even more important one, for the gulf between the associative powers of the Hebrew imagination and that of the Greek lay in their respective religions. To the earlier Hebrews the gods of the Homeric epics, had they known of them in their tight, isolated land, would have seemed as abhorrent as they did seem when, in their later years as a subject nation, they came under the sway of Alexander's Empire and began their series of bitter struggles against the Hellenistic religious and moral ideas and customs forced upon them by their conquerors. Gods who came and went from snowy Olympus in one disguise after another, now as an eagle, now as a beggar, now as a valued friend; who quarreled among themselves; who were as vain and capricious as mortals and subject to mortal desires and even lusts;— these would have seemed to the people of ancient Israel far more shocking and repulsive even than Chemosh, the god of the Moabites, or Melkart, the god of the Sidonians. Such mortal traits, except in their most primitive times, had no part with their One and Transcendent God, eternal in the heavens and yet never absent from the earthly hopes and anxieties of men.

The Greek gods and goddesses in the hands of Homer provide drama, action, scenes of lust and passion, ceremonials, wrath, irony, humor, and long passages of description. Think of the pages given to the design and decoration on the shield of Achilles, framed by the cunning hands of Hephaestus. They halt the main narrative in countless places. Most of these familiar Homeric literary devices were as unknown to the Hebrew writer as were the mortal failings of the immortal gods unknown to him and his people.

It was from this very conception of their God that their associative powers of imagination inevitably received deepest impetus and expression. He did not so much encircle their ways from the beginning as He surrounded them with those defenses and towers dear to the imagination of the Psalmists; every act of their existence as a people was not so much enveloped by Him as suffused by the radiance of His presence. He had a concern for all things, from the lowest and most familiar to the highest. In His infinite wisdom and care the nest of the stork in the fir tree and the widow's cruse of oil had as intimate a place as the crossing of the Red Sea or as the return of the exiles from Babylon. Everything in the present had its prototype in the illimitable past and was, therefore, inseparable from it, making mere time only an illusion. The promises made to the patriarchs must inevitably be fulfilled whatever the seeming troubles, backslidings, or fears. When Israel was but a child, as Hosea affirms and re-affirms, God led him by the hand, and He will lead him still. The pillar of cloud by day and of fire by night is eternally present in those innumerable lights in the darkness which illuminate the imagery of Hebrew poetry. Always to the prophets a "remnant" is to be saved, to return, and to come again unto Zion. To see things as they *are* meant to the Hebrew imagination to see them as they had always been, their seeming outward forms forever endowed with significance and meaning, born of memory and of measureless association.

Thus to that imagination all things belonged together, bound by a fathomless past and a limitless future. And it was this very fact which lent to its associative powers both depth and vastness. "The true and distinctive greatness of Holy Scripture," writes Eric Auerbach in his remarkable book *Mimesis*, "is that it created an entirely new kind of sublimity in which the everyday and the low were included, so that, in style and content, it directly connected the lowest with the highest." A hundred proofs of this statement spring to one's mind. The familiar mountains which rise around Jerusalem become as the Lord who "is round about his people henceforth and even forever." As the rain and the snow from heaven "give seed to the sower and bread to the eater," so is God's word which goeth out of His mouth. David will not drink the water from the well at Bethlehem for which he has longed, but when his three soldiers have brought it to him, he pours it out unto the Lord, for they have risked their lives to get it for him. Elisha does not consider the borrowed axe-head of an anxious man beneath his miraculous powers. The thirsty hart which longs for the brooks of water is the human soul longing for God. "As a hiding-place from the wind" shall a man be; yet a shadow signifies his days; and the entire round of his birth and death is but "as water spilt upon the ground."

To its power of association the imagination of the Old Testament writers adds an intensity of emotion which arouses imaginative sympathy in the minds of their readers by its very force and strength. This emotion, real, spontaneous, and infectious, convinces the reader that it is his own, not only that of the artist. Whether the Psalmist writes of the rivers of Babylon, or the Second Isaiah of the lame man who shall leap and of the dumb who shall sing, or the poet of Job of the grave wherein both kings of the earth and prisoners rest together, our world is suddenly widened to admit them all. It is never another world to which we are taken through the pages of the Old Testament. Homer takes us to Ithaca or to Phaeacia or to the plains of Troy; but the Old Testament narrator and poet take us only to the farthest limits of our own experience. They endow the familiar, homely things which we have always known with a significance unrecognized before; the people with whom we live, with ageless emotions common to us all. By a word, a phrase, the fall of a line they sharpen the pattern of life which we know, add to its design, its color, its truth. Thus the world in which we live is clarified, heightened, recreated through our own imaginative sympathy, even through our identification with that ancient, timeless world of which we read. We sell our birthrights in a hundred ways; covet our neighbor's vineyards; set forth on endless, undefined journeys; make our beds in Hell; find our friends physicians of no value; and at rare moments of vision discover the dwelling-place of light.

Can we, then, doubt that the Old Testament from beginning to end is the work of religious imagination? And that this imagination lies behind and within all its tradition, its history, even its Law? Through the strange, identifying power of that imagination its history becomes a universal history, the story of mankind from the beginning of time to its end. Its emotions cease to be those of individuals living at any certain age or in any certain place, but become instead the accumulated, changeless emotions of countless generations. Its Law in its highest sense is but the restless, imperfect, eternal strivings of the human soul after righteousness.

The peculiar task of the religious imagination is to reveal, however dimly, the nature of the divine mystery. Yet the divine mystery, as the writers of the Old Testament understood, is at the same time the mystery of the world and of the life of man. Must it not then be the mystery of the real, or the mystery forever within things as they *are?*

3
Greek and Hebrew
Story-Tellers

ALTHOUGH the ancient story-tellers of Greece and of her islands and those living at much the same time among the hills of Canaan were, so far as we know, completely unaware of one another, they possessed in common many similar ideas and points of view. Both were seemingly prompted by the same desires and concerned with much the same general material. Both were keenly aware of the traditions of their respective peoples, knew how these traditions were woven into thoughts and memories, and had, as doubtless their first impetus toward writing, the desire to preserve them.

Although their times seem ancient to us in the twentieth century, their world was already old. They must have realized even in their day that what we now call folklore was in its essence the ways and even the necessities of a people. They understood that it was far more than mere tales and legends; that instead it centered around and tried to answer the eternal questions of simple people about the origins of the world, the means of life, the beginnings of races, the source of human pain. They knew, in brief, that such stories are not simply charming in themselves, but that they are basic to a people's existence since they arise not only from national and racial loyalty, but also from a universal curiosity about the mystery of human existence, the sorrows of human life. Such perceptions on the part of these ancient writers are quite evident in many passages both in the Greek epics and in the Old Testament. Achilles says to Priam, the father of Hector, that the life of man by the mysterious decrees of the gods is destined for sorrow, and the writer of the 3rd chapter of Genesis echoes his understanding.

The most brilliantly told legend among the Hebrew narratives, that of Jacob and Joseph, contained in Genesis, chapters 27 to 50, inclusive, is perhaps more accurately termed a *saga* since it deals with family relationships and is, first of all, a human rather than a national document. Nevertheless, it possesses distinctly epical qualities like those of the *Iliad* and the *Odyssey*. It is an heroic story, the characters of which are the descendants of Abraham and Isaac, and, therefore, in the Hebrew mind the founders of its tribes and the preservers of its race. It is animated throughout by racial pride and patriotic fervor, emotions common to the Greek, and, of course, to all epics.

The *Iliad* and the *Odyssey* and the Jacob-Joseph saga contain alike themes common to most ancient literature. Odysseus and Jacob are both men who escape from perils and who are wanderers; both return home after long years away. In both the Hebrew saga and the Greek epics are familiar motifs. There are dreams which reveal the truth like the dreams of the chief baker and the chief butler, interpreted by Joseph in prison, like Pharaoh's dream of the fat and the lean kine, and like Penelope's dream of the geese and the eagle; and the origin of these dreams is accorded to God or to the gods. There is in both Greek and Hebrew stories the sense of obligation to the stranger; there is the giving of gifts, Jacob's gifts which he plans for Esau, Joseph's gifts to his brothers; and the innumerable gifts which fill the pages of the *Iliad* and the *Odyssey*. There is the time-worn old motif of disguise, in Rebekah's disguise of Jacob so that his father may think he is Esau and in the many instances of disguise in the epics, from the various disguises of the gods and goddesses, who appear in any number of forms, to Odysseus' final disguise as a beggar in tattered rags when he returns at last to Ithaca and plans with the help of Athene to rid his house of the wooers of Penelope who have despoiled it. There are bargainings and tricks and cleverness, whether it is Jacob's shrewdness in gaining Laban's flocks for himself, or Odysseus' desperate cunning in the cave of Polyphemus, the Cyclops. There are touching revelations like that of the final revelation of Joseph to his wondering brothers, or of Odysseus when the old nurse Eurycleia in giving him his bath sees the scar from the tusk of the wild boar. And although the story of Jacob and Joseph is one of peace and that of the *Iliad* and, in retrospect, of the *Odyssey* one of war, the atmosphere of both Hebrew and Greek narratives takes us back to the beginnings of things, even although it is a different beginning, and to the portrayal of basic, primitive, changeless human emotions and passions: fear, rage, jealousy, lust, revenge, love, and hatred.

II

But once we have noted the similarities in these ancient stories, each of the childhood of a race, we must become keenly alive to their sharp and pronounced differences, both in form and in methods of literary creation. For in these differences lie not only the singularity of the Hebrew story-tellers, their distinction from all others of any race and time, but, indeed, those characteristics which have marked through centuries the distinction between the Greek literary legacy to Western culture and that of the Hebrew. In studying these differences there is a practical and utilitarian value to the reader of the Old Testament, for in understanding them he becomes more clearly aware of how its narratives must be read in order to gain from them their meaning and significance, quite lost to him without that knowledge.

The first and most obvious difference between the literary conceptions and methods of the Greek and the Hebrew writers lies in the length which they respectively accord to their stories. The *Iliad*, somewhat longer than the *Odyssey* in its number of lines, consists of twenty-four books; the *Odyssey* of an equal number. The Jacob-Joseph saga in its entirety, that is, from the blessing of Isaac to the death of Jacob in Egypt and his burial in the Land of Canaan, comprises thirty-four chapters, and of that number two should be omitted as having no bearing on the story itself.[2] Indeed, the complete epic, or saga, of Jacob and Joseph could be put into any one of the longer books of the *Iliad* or the *Odyssey*.

The reason for this immense disparity in size lies, first, in the *brevity* characteristic of the Hebrew story-tellers, and, second, in the *principle of omission*, a practice always employed by them. These two literary traits mark all early Old Testament narratives. They are as evident in the account of David's court and in the isolated hero stories as they are in the Jacob-Joseph saga. For the employment of the first of these, *brevity*, and its consequent literary and imaginative effects, let us compare Homer's presentation of certain characters in terms of their background and appearance with that of the Hebrew writers.

Homer's great figures always come from some clearly identified place. Helen, the cause of the Trojan War, whose face in Marlowe's words

> *launched a thousand ships*
> *And burnt the topless towers of Ilium,*

comes from Sparta where, before Paris lured her away, she was the wife of King Menelaus. Andromache, the beautiful wife of Hector, comes from Thebe. The home of Odysseus is in sea-girt Ithaca, but we are told carefully that his grandparents lived at Parnassus. When Achilles, once having overcome his wrath at Agamemnon, proceeds to make

[2] We must realize, of course, that the Biblical stories in their original form were not divided into chapters as we know them.

havoc among the heroes of Troy, either he takes time before his slaughter of them to ask their homes and their lineage or Homer himself discloses their places of birth and their noble parentage.

In contrast we are told practically nothing of those equally great figures who live and move in the ancient Hebrew saga. Their dwelling-places are never described in even the least detail and often not clearly identified. Apparently Isaac lived at Beersheba, or the *Well of the Oath*, when, old and blind, he was tricked into blessing Jacob instead of the rightful Esau; yet the selling of the birthright, which preceded the blessing, seems to have been near some other well where he had pitched his tent. The time and place of the most important happenings are alike undefined. Are Haran and Padan-aram the same place? They would seem to be from the account in Genesis, and yet one was clearly a town and the other a district. And in what places did Jacob stop on that long journey from Beersheba to Haran? Not one except Bethel is identified although the journey must have occupied many days. We are told only that he went on his journey and came into the land of the people of the east.

Both Odysseus and Jacob spent twenty years away from home, Odysseus on his wanderings, Jacob in the service of Laban. The places of Odysseus' wanderings, as he sails from one to another, are always both named and carefully described: Ogygia, the far-off isle of Calypso; the land of the Phaeacians, who need no rudders for their ships; the drowsy land of the Lotus Eaters and that of the Cyclopes, who dwell in hollow caves; the isle of Circe; and the dreadful Charybdis and Scylla. Jacob presumably wandered a great deal during his long term of service with Laban, since he was a shepherd; but if he did, we know little or nothing about it. We are told once only that he removed himself with his speckled and spotted flocks "a three days' journey" from Laban, but to what place we do not know. Nor are the various stages named of the return journey which he took with his household when he determined to flee from Padan-aram to the Land of Canaan. He is at Mt. Gilead; he wrestles with the angel of God at a place which, in commemoration, he himself names Peniel; he continues to Succoth; then suddenly he is at Shechem in the very land of Canaan. From there, after the sorry tragedy of his daughter Dinah, he seemingly moves on to Bethel and beyond; and yet he is apparently also at Shechem, or at least his flocks are there. Again, time is as if it were not, and place is rarely identified.

Homer describes in careful detail the houses in which people lived. King Priam had a beautiful palace, adorned with polished colonnades, in which were fifty chambers of polished stone. The bronze walls of King Alcinous' house in Phaeacia gave forth a gleam like that of the sun or the moon; round them was a frieze of blue; the doors were of gold and the door-posts of silver; and without the courtyard was a great garden with hedges and fruit trees. Penelope's chamber in Odysseus' great house in Ithaca was reached by a tall staircase, and in the "uttermost part" of the house was a treasure room, the oaken threshold of which had been "planed cunningly by the carpenter."

Such description as this is unimaginable in the Old Testament. The patriarchs "pitch their tents" wherever they find food and water; people in the small Canaanitish villages often, like Rahab, live on the town wall. We are told that the carpenters and masons of Hiram, king of Tyre, built David a house of cedar, but we have no idea what it was like any more than we can picture Solomon's house, which, with his other glories, made the Queen of Sheba breathless. Amos condemns the people of the north for their winter houses and their summer houses, and also for their houses of ivory, but they are only mentioned, never described or located. In the very late book of Esther, which shows various foreign influences, we *are* told of a few elegant furnishings in the palace at Shushan, but this is the one exception. The only house in the Old Testament described in detail is the House of God, the Temple built by Solomon in Jerusalem.

Homer pictures all his characters. His heroes, their hair, their eyes, their stature, their clothing and armor—all receive his utmost care. He is especially susceptible to the charms of his women, whether born of gods or of mortals; and although he pictures them in far less detail than his heroes, each possesses a special grace. Who can forget the white-armed Nausicaa, the daughter of King Alcinous, whose form and comeliness are like to the immortals and who in Odysseus' ravished eyes is like a young palm tree springing by the altar of Apollo in Delos? Odysseus' old nurse, Eurycleia, with her stumbling feet and uncertain hands still holds a graciousness which no age can wither. When she discerns the scar which proves that she is, in very truth, bathing her master and lord, she lets his foot drop so suddenly in her agitation that the water is spilled on the ground. And although Sir Gilbert Murray insists that Helen is described with great restraint in the *Iliad*,[3] she is, in comparison with any woman in the Old Testament, very clearly seen. She may claim that she is but a *dog* to have caused the war between the Greeks and the Trojans; but her enchantment is quite evident to herself as to us when she sits in her chamber in her perfumed raiment with her beautiful hair and in her hands the web of purple wool which she is embroidering with the battles she has caused men to fight. We see her also weeping in her white veil much as the elders on the wall of Troy saw her when they said to one another: "Small wonder that the Trojans and mailed Greeks should endure pain through many years for such a woman!"

It is almost impossible to see any Old Testament character in terms of physical features or of dress. David is perhaps

[3] In *The Rise of the Greek Epic*, pp. 253-54.

an exception since he is accorded two adjectives instead of one: he is ruddy, that is, red-haired, and of a beautiful countenance. Samson has heavy hair, but that feature is stressed, clearly because in his hair lay the secret of his strength. Absalom is said to be beautiful, "without blemish from the sole of his foot even to the crown of his head." His hair, too, like Samson's is extraordinary, nearly nine pounds in weight at its yearly cutting, but it, too, is obviously emphasized only because it is to be the cause of his death. What did Abraham look like, or Isaac, or Jacob? We do not know. Joseph has a coat of many colors and apparently at seventeen a manner which infuriates his half-brothers, but except for these details and the fact that Potiphar's wife in Egypt thought him well-favored, he is likewise impossible to visualize.

The women who play such dramatic parts not only in the Jacob-Joseph saga, but throughout the Old Testament narratives are almost never made visible by any definite physical features. Bathsheba, who caused such tragedy, is described only as "very beautiful to look upon" at that fatal hour when David from his roof saw her bathing. We can only imagine what Rebekah with her ruthless cunning must have looked like. Jael, the slayer of Sisera, is presented only in fierce action; Hagar only weeping over her little son in the wilderness. Sarah, whom we remember most clearly for her ironic laughter, is "very fair," so fair, indeed, that Abraham fears for his own life at the hand of the covetous Pharaoh and therefore determines to tell the king that she is his sister. Leah and Rachel, most important among Hebrew women because they are the mothers of the tribes of Israel, are contrasted in appearance: "Leah was tender-eyed; but Rachel was beautiful and well-favored." The Jewish translation is more true to the original Hebrew than is the King James in its description of the first wife of Jacob. Leah had *weak*, or sore eyes; and this unfortunate blemish is perhaps one reason why she was less attractive to Jacob than was the beautiful Rachel.

It is, however, in the portrayal of human emotions that the Greek epics show the greatest difference from the Hebrew stories. In both, these emotions are basic, instinctive, and natural; but the presentation of them is in direct contrast. In illustration of this marked difference, let us compare the manner in which the Greek and the Hebrew writers relate the effects of grief.

Tears in Homer are most common. Even the horses of Patroclus weep and mourn for him, trailing their manes on the ground in sorrow. When Odysseus, disguised from Penelope, tells her "false tales in the likeness of truth," her tears flow

> even as the snow melts in the high places of the hills, the snow that the southeast wind has thawed, and as it wastes, the river streams run full, even so her fair cheeks melted beneath her tears.

Tears, although they are not uncommon to the later Hebrew poets, are never mentioned in the ancient Hebrew narratives. Here people merely weep, and then but seldom. Hannah "wept sore" in the temple at Shiloh; and Esau "lifted up his voice and wept" when he realized that he had been defrauded of his father's blessing. Jonathan and David wept over their common sorrow; and David often wept as he had bitter cause to do. But the verb is commonly used by itself as though its unsupported strength were quite enough.

Scenes of grief, common to both Greek and Old Testament stories, reveal an illimitable distance between the literary methods of their respective narrators. A few of the many among these will suffice as illustrations:

When tidings are brought to Achilles of the death of Patroclus, his friend, he pours dust over his head, disfigures his face, throws himself on the ground, and "with his own hands" tears his hair. He moans so terribly that his mother, Thetis, hears him in her cave in the depths of the sea and comes to his tent to hear his groans, bringing with her a score of Nereids who also add their outcries to the general tumult of grief throughout many pages. When tidings are brought to David of the death of Jonathan, his friend, the Hebrew story-teller thus describes his grief:

> Then David took hold on his clothes and rent them, and likewise all the men that were with him. And

> they mourned and wept and fasted until even, for Saul and for Jonathan his son, and for the people of the Lord, and for the house of Israel, because they were fallen by the sword.
> And David lamented with this lamentation:

> *How are the mighty fallen in the midst of the battle!*
> *O Jonathan, thou wast slain in thy high places!*
> *I am distressed for thee, my brother Jonathan.*
> *Very pleasant hast thou been unto me.*
> *Thy love to me was wonderful,*
> *Passing the love of women.*

Another striking contrast is seen in the behavior and speech of Hecuba, the mother of Hector, when she sees her son dragged in the dust behind the chariot of Achilles and in that of the mother of Sisera when she tries to assure herself that her son yet lives:

> When she beheld her son, his mother, Hecuba, tore her hair and cast far from her her shining veil and cried aloud with an exceeding bitter cry. She led the wild lament among the women of Troy.
> "My child, ah, woe is me! Wherefore should I live in my pain, now that thou art dead, who night and day wert my boast through the city, and blessing to all, both men and women of Troy throughout the town who hailed thee as a god, for verily an exceeding glory to them wert thou in thy life. Now death and fate have overtaken thee."

She continues her lament once Priam has returned home with Hector's body:

"Hector of all my children dearest to my heart,
verily while thou wert alive, dear wert thou to the
gods, and even in thy doom of death have they had
care for thee. For other sons of mine whom he took
captive would fleet Achilles sell beyond the un-
vintaged sea, unto Samos and Imbros and smoking
Lemnos. But when with keen-edged bronze he had
bereft thee of thy life, he was fain to drag thee oft
around the tomb of his comrade, even Patroclus
whom thou slewest, yet he might not raise him up
thereby. But now all dewy and fresh thou liest in our
halls like one on whom Apollo, lord of the silver
bow, hath descended and slain him with his gentle
darts."

Sisera's mother, of whom we have known nothing earlier, looks out of her window with her anxious ladies. And
as she waits, she mumbles over and over to herself the vain
hope that his chariot is only delayed while the spoils of
battle are divided:

> The mother of Sisera looked out at a window
> And cried through the lattice:
> Why is his chariot so long in coming?
> Why tarry the wheels of his chariots?
> Her wise ladies answered her,
> Yea, she returned answer to herself:
> Have they not sped?
> Have they not divided the prey?
> To every man a damsel or two,
> To Sisera a prey of divers colors,
> A prey of divers colors of needlework,
> Of divers colors of needlework on both sides,
> Meet for the necks of them that take the spoil.

The 23rd book of the *Iliad*, the next to the longest book
in terms of lines, is given over completely to the funeral
of Patroclus, his burial, and the funeral games which follow. Everything in the 897 lines used for the description
is related in the utmost detail: the gathering of the wood

for the funeral pyre; the procession of chariots and the numberless footmen; the cuttings of hair to be strewn over the body as symbols of grief; the body of Patroclus borne by his comrades and his head carried by Achilles; the golden lock from Achilles' head which he cuts and places in the hand of Patroclus; the building of the great pyre a hundred feet in height; the prayers to the winds to ignite the fire; the gathering of Patroclus' bones in a golden urn for burial. And all these events *before* the funeral games which go on interminably.

No account could be farther from this, both in matter and manner, than that related in the last chapter of I Samuel of the treatment accorded to the bodies of Saul and Jonathan:

> And it came to pass on the morrow, when the Philistines came to strip the slain, that they found Saul and his three sons fallen in Mt. Gilboa. And they cut off his head and stripped off his armor and sent into the land of the Philistines round about, to publish it in the house of their idols and among the people. And they put his armor in the house of Ashtaroth, and they fastened his body to the wall of Bethshan.
>
> And when the inhabitants of Jabesh-Gilead heard of that which the Philistines had done to Saul, all the valiant men arose and went all night, and took the body of Saul and the bodies of his sons from the wall of Bethshan and came to Jabesh, and burnt them there. And they took their bones and buried them under a tree at Jabesh, and fasted seven days.

But perhaps the most clear and most noteworthy contrast both in method and in atmosphere is the grief displayed by Priam over the death of Hector, his son, and that shown by David over the death of Absalom. The scene between Priam and Achilles in the last book of the *Iliad* is, of course, one of the most beautiful and moving scenes in any literature of any time and should be read in its perfect wholeness instead of in the much abbreviated excerpt given here. Priam, guided by Hermes, has come to beg from Hector's slayer the body of his son:

The old man made straight for the house where Achilles, dear to Zeus, was wont to sit; and therein he found Achilles himself. And Priam clasped in his hands the knees of Achilles and kissed his hands, terrible, man-slaying, that slew many of Priam's sons. And Achilles wondered when he saw god-like Priam. Then Priam spoke and entreated him, saying:

"Bethink thee, O Achilles like to gods, of *thy* father that is of like years with me, on the grievous pathway of old age. While he heareth of thee as yet alive, he rejoiceth in his heart, and hopeth withal day after day that he shall see his dear son returning from Troy-land. But I, I am utterly unblest, since I begat some of the best men in wide Troy-land; but I declare unto thee that none of them is left. Fifty I had when the sons of the Achaeans came; nineteen were born to me of one mother, and concubines bare the rest within my walls. The only one yet left who guarded city and men, him thou slewest but now, as he fought for his country, even Hector. For his sake I come unto the ships of the Achaeans that I may win him back from thee, and I bring with me untold ransoms. Yea, fear thou the gods, Achilles, and have compassion on me, even me, bethinking thee of thy father. Lo, I am yet more piteous than he, and hath braved what none other man on earth hath braved before, to stretch forth my hand toward the slayer of my sons."

Thus spake he, and stirred within Achilles desire to make lament for his father. And he touched the old man's hand and gently moved him back. And as they both bethought them of their dead, so Priam for Hector wept sore, and Achilles wept for his own father, and now again for Patroclus, and their moan went up throughout the house. But when noble Achilles had satisfied him with lament, straightway he sprang from his seat and raised the old man by his hand, pitying his hoary head and hoary beard, and spake unto him winged words, and said:

"Ah, hapless one! Many ill things verily thou hast endured in thy heart. How durst thou come alone to the ships of the Achaeans to meet the eyes of the man who hath slain full many of thy brave sons? Of iron verily is thy heart. But come then, set thee on a seat, and we will let our sorrows lie quiet in our hearts."

Then made answer unto him the old man, god-like Priam:

"Bid me not to a seat, O fosterling of Zeus, so long as Hector lieth uncared for; but straightway give him back that I may behold him with mine eyes; and accept thou the great ransom that we bring. So mayest thou have pleasure thereof, and come into thy native land."

Then Achilles, the son of Peleus, leapt like a lion through the door of the house, not alone, for with him went two squires. They then loosed from under the yoke the horses and mules of Priam, and from the train they took the countless ransom set on Hector's head. But they left two robes and a well-spun doublet that Achilles might wrap the dead therein when he gave him to his father to be carried home. So when the handmaids had washed the body of Hector and anointed it with oil and had thrown over it a fair robe and a doublet, then Achilles himself lifted it and laid it on a bier, and his comrades with him lifted it onto the wagon.

Then Achilles went back into the hut and spake a word to Priam:

"Thy son, old sire, is given back as thou wouldest and lieth on a bier, and with the break of day thou shalt see him thyself as thou carriest him. But come, say this to me and tell it true, how many days' space thou art fain to make funeral for noble Hector, so that for so long I may myself abide and may keep back the host. For I will hold back the battle even so long a time as thou tellest me."

Thus speaking, he clasped the old man's right hand at the wrist, lest he should be anywise afraid at heart.

The unknown Hebrew chronicler who, in perhaps the same century, described another bitter grief, could not, because of his own racial temperament and his own language, draw his scene after the manner of Homer. Yet with all its brevity, understatement, and lack of detail, it, too, holds its secure place as an unexcelled piece of literary art:

And David sat between the two gates. And the watchman went up to the roof over the gate unto the wall, and lifted up his eyes and looked, and behold a man running alone. And the watchman cried and told the king. And the king said, If he be alone, there is tidings in his mouth. And he came apace, and drew near.

And the watchman saw another man running. And the watchman called unto the porter, and said, Behold another man running alone. And the king said, He also bringeth tidings. And the watchman said, Methinketh the running of the foremost is like the running of Ahimaaz the son of Zadok. And the king said, He is a good man, and cometh with good tidings.

And Ahimaaz called, and said unto the king, All is well. And he fell down to the earth upon his face before the king, and said, Blessed be the Lord thy God, which hath delivered up the men that lifted up their hand against my lord the king! And the king said, Is the young man Absalom safe? And Ahimaaz answered, When Joab sent the king's servant and me, thy servant, I saw a great tumult, but I knew not what it was. And the king said unto him, Turn aside, and stand here. And he turned aside, and stood still.

And behold Cushi came. And Cushi said, Tidings, my lord the king; for the Lord hath avenged thee this day of all them that rose up against thee. And the king said unto Cushi, Is the young man Absalom safe? And Cushi said, The enemies of my lord the king, and all that rise against thee to do thee hurt, be as that young man is.

And the king was much moved, and went up to the chamber over the gate, and wept. And as he went, thus he said:

O my son Absalom, my son, my son Absalom!
Would God I had died for thee, O Absalom, my
son, my son!

III

The Hebrew story-teller differed from the Greek not
only in his almost laconic *brevity* and in his total lack of
all but the most indispensable detail, but also in his seemingly careful use of *omission* as a literary method and even
principle. Homer leaves no gaps to fill, no wide bridges to
span. We know every stage on his journeys; every thought
in the minds of his people; every emotion felt by them with
all its outward and visible signs. In contrast, the Hebrew
narrator deals in empty spaces.

This omission in the telling of Old Testament stories is
very similar to that constantly employed by the unknown
composers of the English and Scottish popular ballads. The
original writers of *The Wife of Usher's Well* or of *Sir
Patrick Spens* depend upon the imagination of their hearers
or readers, and therein lies much of the charm of their old
tales. Each of us evolves his own picture of the carline wife
of Usher's well, whatever and wherever that was, and of
her three "stout and stalwart" sons whom she sent over
the sea. For what reason she sent them we are not told,
nor do we know how they met their deaths. When they
return to her as ghosts, does she see that their hats are of
the tree that grows only in Paradise? Is the crowing of the
"red, red cock" and that of the gray which hurry them
back to their graves the result of her terrible curse? And
what is the relation between them and that "bonny lass"
who kindles their mother's fire and to whom they bid their
last farewells? We know none of the answers, nor do we
want to know them.

The same omissions mark *Sir Patrick Spens*. He is at
one moment walking on the sand; at the next he is calling to his merry men to launch the king's ship; and at the

last he with his men are fifty fathoms deep at the bottom of the sea with their plumed hats floating above them. Just what happened in the days between these momentous events is anyone's guess. The ballad writers go at once to the heart of the matter, ruthlessly omitting what in their minds is unnecessary.

In like manner the Hebrew story-tellers are constantly leaving important events and more important emotions in complete obscurity. Just as time and place are undefined, so thoughts and feelings are unexpressed, suggested only by emptiness and silence or by the most fragmentary speeches. Yet this method of narration results in a dramatic suspense impossible in Homer.

Questions constantly rise in our minds as we read these ancient stories. Who were the "wise ladies" of Sisera's mother? Did they sit like the ladies in *Sir Patrick Spens*, waiting for tidings, with their gold combs in their hair? Did Uriah the Hittite have the least suspicion that he bore his own death concealed in David's letter to Joab? What did Heber the Kenite say to Jael, his wife, when he learned of her terrible act against his new allies? What had been the deeply laid plans between the desperate mother of Moses and his frightened sister, who stood afar off and watched the baby in his cradle of bulrushes? What did Joseph's half-brothers say about him around their sheep-folds by night? Surely they did not confine themselves only to their scornful, "Behold, this dreamer cometh!" That was but the climax of their irritation and jealousy.

These many empty spaces in the Old Testament, these bare, unfurnished rooms, these uncompleted designs and patterns arouse curiosity and wonder in the reader's mind. And nowhere are they better illustrated than in the 22nd chapter of Genesis, which gives the account of the sacrifice of Isaac:

> And it came to pass after these things that God did tempt Abraham, and said unto him, Abraham; and

he said, Behold, here I am. And he said, Take now
thy son, thine only son Isaac, whom thou lovest, and
get thee unto the land of Moriah; and offer him there
for a burnt offering upon one of the mountains
which I will tell thee of.

And Abraham rose up early in the morning, and
saddled his ass, and took two of his young men with
him, and Isaac his son, and clave the wood for the
burnt offering, and rose up, and went unto the place
of which God had told him.

Then on the third day Abraham lifted up his eyes,
and saw the place afar off.

And Abraham said unto his young men, Abide ye
here with the ass; and I and the lad will go yonder
and worship, and come again to you.

And Abraham took the wood of the burnt offering
and laid it upon Isaac his son; and he took the fire in
his hand, and a knife; and they went both of them together. And Isaac spake unto Abraham his father,
and said, My father; and he said, Here am I, my son.
And he said, Behold the fire and the wood, but where
is the lamb for a burnt offering? And Abraham said,
My son, God will provide a lamb for a burnt offering. So they went both of them together.

And they came to the place which God had told
him of; and Abraham built an altar there, and laid the
wood in order, and bound Isaac his son, and laid
him on the altar upon the wood. And Abraham
stretched forth his hand, and took the knife to slay
his son.

And the angel of the Lord called unto him out of
heaven, and said, Abraham, Abraham; and he said,
Here am I. And he said, Lay not thine hand upon
the lad, neither do thou anything unto him. For now
I know that thou fearest God, seeing thou hast not
withheld thy son, thine only son from me.

And Abraham lifted up his eyes, and looked, and
behold behind him a ram caught in a thicket by his
horns; and Abraham went and took the ram, and
offered him up for a burnt offering in the stead of
his son.

The power of this perfectly told story lies in its omissions, in what is not said, in its terrible silence and desolation. Where are Abraham and God when the awful command is given? What had been "these things" after which it comes to pass? What do we know of Isaac? Since he was clearly old enough to carry the wood for the burnt offering when he and his father left the young men and went on "both of them together," he must have had his own questions in his mind; yet he speaks but once. He is silent when his father binds him and lays him upon the altar. We know nothing of him, except that his father loves him as his only son. Perhaps we are supposed to understand, as doubtless those who first heard the story did understand, that in Isaac alone lay the future of the race. Perhaps it may also occur to us that there is bitter irony in the meaning of Isaac's name, *laughter*. Since Abraham rose up early in the morning to make the careful, simple preparations for his journey, God may have appeared to him in the darkness. What of the night before, and what of the three days on the way? Not a suggestion is given us of Abraham's grief and terror. We know only that on the third day he lifted up his eyes and saw the place afar off.

The bareness of this story like so many others in the Old Testament possesses more than it can ever impart, means more than it can ever say. It is like the scattered stones of some ancient, once carefully wrought building, now in ruins, like Stonehenge, or the temple of Aesculapius at Epidaurus, or of Poseidon at Sunion. The stones stand about in the grass with wide spaces between them, each once a part of a whole, yet each more full of meaning in its very solitude. We can reconstruct the building if we like, but many of us will not wish to do so, seeing in the single stones an indefinable charm, nameless and ageless, which the completed building could never convey, regardless of its beauty.

IV

To readers like myself, devoted both to the Homeric epics and to the Old Testament narratives, it is difficult to conceive of literary styles and treatments more different in every respect. The former, with their atmosphere of leisure, their lack of suspense, their fluency, elaboration, and ornament, their complete expression of emotion, stand in direct contrast to the latter, almost even in alienation from them. The Hebrew writers know nothing of the sophistication of the Greek. The language which they employed for their stories was sharp and quick, unfinished, inflexible, fragmentary in comparison; the emotions which it suggested were never fully described. And yet, through its very brevity and bareness and through its empty silences, its writers were able to evoke responses and even understandings impossible to the writers of the epics. Since the Homeric poets reveal everything, conceal nothing, they trail few invisible meanings within their thousands of beautiful phrases and intricate, detailed similes.

The imagination plays around the scenes in the *Iliad* and the *Odyssey* as in a spectrum of light and color; but it rarely leaves them. It is tethered by details; all its questions are answered; it is allowed no mysterious flights of its own. Homer can be analyzed, but he offers small room for interpretation. The Greek epics are ancient poems, but they are not timeless in the Hebraic sense. Their magnificent heroes, though some of them are of immortal birth, are yet mortal and individual; around them is no sense of the universal. Their time has a discernible beginning, a sure and certain end; it is not from everlasting to everlasting. The wanderings of Odysseus begin from Troy and end in Ithaca, whereas the wanderings of the patriarchs, by their peculiar power of association and identification, forever suggest the wanderings of all men in search of God.

4
Imaginative Ideas in the Old Testament

R EADERS of the Old Testament are sure to be impressed before they proceed very far into its pages by the constant presence of the most concrete and simple objects and occupations: bread, butter, cakes, honey, milk, water, wine, oil; oxen, goats, kids, asses, mules, sheep, and lambs; ploughing, sowing, threshing, sickling, pruning, gleaning, harvesting; the moulding of clay, the weaving of cloth, the cooking and eating of food, the shearing of sheep. The reiteration of these familiar objects and pursuits is in no sense unusual, of course, to any ancient and primarily agricultural people; but the distinctive way in which each of these concrete images is repeatedly used *is* unusual and a proof of Eric Auerbach's statement that the everyday and the low are always invested with sublimity by the Old Testament writers.

The Hebrew mind, as we have seen, was itself concrete and intrinsically realistic. Yet the associative powers of that mind and its intensely emotional character were perpetually endowing the simple and the obvious with their inner and spiritual significance, forever transcending the familiar and the ordinary. Thus the literal becomes the figurative as well; the concrete loses its sharp outlines in the abstract. Nothing is seen alone, but is forever attended by its meaning, like a surrounding light or a reflected shadow.

This power of transcending the ordinary, of endowing it with imaginative significance, is most clearly illustrated, perhaps, in the treatment throughout the Old Testament of the parts of the human body. A singular sensitiveness to the physical was without doubt closely related to the vitality of the ancient Hebrews as a race and also to the hardihood and resiliency required of them, both by their background and by their history. But whatever its source, the perpetual reference in the Old Testament to parts of the body can hardly escape one's notice. Poets, prophets, and narrators alike write of these: of the head, neck, eyes, mouth, teeth, tongue, arms, legs, fingers and toes, and even knees. They write often of the heart and the ears also; but these organs are generally used in a figurative sense as the sources of feeling and of understanding. Bones claim their interest; and although the term is frequently used for the whole body, or, in Ezekiel's famous vision of the valley of bones as the whole house of Israel, it is just as often used concretely and sometimes specifically: the thighbone, the jawbone, the rib, or even the fifth rib, which was carefully located as the fatal goal for the thrusts of Abner and of Joab.

Not infrequently these bodily members are employed most effectively to describe emotion. When Eliphaz, the friend of Job, sees a spirit passing in the night before his eyes, all his bones shake in terror, and the hairs on his skin stand up. Job says bitterly that his enemies express their scorn of him by gnashing their teeth and by sharpening their eyes upon him, and that God has taken him by his neck and shaken him to pieces. He describes his despair by saying that his bones burn with heat and that his bowels boil. The anger of both kings and ordinary men is shown by the stiffening of their necks. The joints of King Belshazzar's loins are loosed when he sees the fingers writing upon the palace wall at his feast, and his knees smite against each other. A wicked man is described in Proverbs as one who "winketh with his eyes, and speaketh with his feet, and teacheth with his fingers." Joseph's bowels yearn when he sees his brother Benjamin. Even God's lips are full of indignation, and His tongue is a devouring fire.

But of all parts of the body none is used so often or with such effectiveness as are *hands* and *feet*. Hands add concreteness to literally hundreds of passages although no reference to them is necessary to the actual meaning of the text. They are surely used deliberately in order to gain this concreteness and distinction. God delivers not simply to Noah's care, but into his *hand* all the beasts of the field and the fowls of the air. Jacob in his reproaches to Laban speaks not only of his labor in the drought by day and the frost by night, but of the labor of his *hands*. Pharaoh leaves all his responsibilities not to Joseph, but in Joseph's *hand*. One is rarely in the Old Testament delivered only from his enemies, but also from their *hands*, just as all the enemies are given over into the *hands* of their conquerors. God tells Hagar to lift up her little boy and hold him in her *hand*.

The work of one's hands, both of those of men and of God, are repeatedly extolled in Hebrew poetry. In the Apocrypha the most ordinary of human occupations are dignified by being understood as a form of prayer:

The wisdom of the scribe cometh by opportunity of leisure.
How shall he become wise that holdeth the plough?
That driveth oxen and is occupied in their labors?
So is the smith, sitting by the anvil
And considering the unwrought iron;
So is the potter, sitting at his work
And turning the wheel about with his feet.
All these put their trust in their hands,
And each becometh wise in his own work.
Without these shall not a city be inhabited.
They shall not be sought for in the council of the people;
They shall not sit on the seat of the judge.
But they will maintain the fabric of the world;
And in the work of their hands is their prayer.

God's hands have not only prepared the dry land, in their

hollows measured the waters, and placed their works in
the firmament of heaven; but they constantly strengthen
and make whole the weak hands of men. His faithful
people are the work of His hands, as well as are the glories
of the sun and the moon; and when He openeth His hand,
He "satisfieth the desire of every living thing."

Countless references are likewise made to *feet* in the Old
Testament; but one is at once aware that these references are
of a far different nature from those having to do with hands.
Feet are rarely accorded the concreteness given to hands.
They are seldom used at all in a literal sense except when
they describe lameness like that of the son of Jonathan, or
the swiftness of foot of those who run, or occur in the
common gesture of one falling before the feet of another.
They are, instead, practically always used in a connotative,
imaginative sense, which is peculiarly moving in its effect
and appeal. Thus they become *ideas* rather than parts of
the human body.

The reasons for this endowment of a man's feet with
special significance lie, it would seem, both in their ancient
connection with religious tradition and, even more im-
portantly, with the part played by them in the long history
of the Hebrew race. To cast the shoes from off one's feet,
as Moses was commanded to do as he approached the burning bush, was an act of reverence and worship, just as to
wash the feet of a guest, wayfarer, or stranger was a sign
or gesture of hospitality and even of humility on the part
of a host. Far older than religious tradition, however, lay
the relation of human feet to human wanderings. To a
desert and nomadic people like the ancient Hebrews, especially to one gifted with their imaginative powers, it seems
natural that feet should early become an idea and a symbol
rather than merely a physical possession. It was their feet
upon which their race had wandered across the deserts
through succeeding generations, which had brought them
up out of Egypt, through the wilderness, and at last into

their Promised Land; their feet which led or followed their flocks over their barren, rocky hills and which meant their means of safety and even of life itself.

It is not surprising, then, to find human feet the subject of many passages in the most exalted of Hebrew poetry. In constant remembrance of the rough and perilous roads over which bare or sandaled feet must walk, the poets see them as slipping or stumbling, or falling into snares and nets, or bruised and weary. The Psalmists cry that they had well-nigh slipped, had not God delivered their feet from falling and in His mercy upheld them. God again rescues the feet of the despairing wayfarer from miry clay and sets them safely upon a rock. His angels bear up in their hands him who makes the Most High his refuge, lest at any time his foot is dashed against a stone.

In the words of Second Isaiah Zion is the place of the feet of God, His sanctuary which He will make "glorious"; and to this poet the feet of him that bringeth good tidings are exalted even above the tidings themselves:

> *How beautiful upon the mountains*
> *Are the feet of him that bringeth good tidings,*
> *That publisheth peace!*
> *That bringeth good tidings of good,*
> *That publisheth salvation!*

In the final chapter of Ecclesiastes the parts of the human body are seen as symbols of the frailty and weakness of old age. The poet here identifies them not in their physical forms, but rather in terms of symbolic images. The hands become the keepers of the house of the body, although they can no longer be trusted to draw water at the well or care for the lamps and the pitchers; the eyes are those that look out at windows; the teeth are grinders; the white hair is the blossoming almond tree; the feet are the fears of high places and of crowded ways. In this late book of the Old Testament this poem in a satisfying way draws together

all the many references made throughout its earlier books
to the human body and its members and endows them with
dignity, if with sadness:

> *In the day when the keepers of the house shall tremble,*
> *And the strong men shall bow themselves,*
> *And the grinders cease because they are few,*
> *And those that look out of the windows be darkened,*
> *The doors shall be shut in the streets*
> *When the sound of the grinding is low,*
> *And he shall rise up at the voice of the bird,*
> *And all the daughters of music shall be brought low.*
> *Also when they shall be afraid of that which is high,*
> *And fears shall be in the way,*
> *And the almond tree shall flourish,*
> *And the grasshopper shall be a burden,*
> *And desire shall fail*
> *Because man goeth to his long home,*
> *And the mourners go about the streets.*
> *Or ever the silver cord be loosed,*
> *Or the golden bowl be broken,*
> *Or the pitcher be broken at the fountain,*
> *Or the wheel broken at the cistern.*
> *Then shall the dust return to the earth as it was,*
> *And the spirit shall return unto God who gave it.*

II

It is an easy transition from the idea of *feet* in the Old
Testament to the idea of the *journeys* which they under-
take. For, after the same manner as the feet themselves,
all wayfaring takes upon itself, through the associative
power of the Hebrew imagination, the impression of a
search or a quest. Also, through his singular emotional
power of identification, the Hebrew writer can throw over
and around these journeys the equally strong impression
that they are not peculiar to one people at one time, but
are instead the ageless experiences of all.

It is significant and perhaps even curious that the Old
Testament is in no sense a book of adventure in the usual
sense of that word. This fact becomes even more striking

when we recall the heroic traits of early Western literature such as the Greek and the Roman epics or the Norse sagas. There are heroes, to be sure, in the Old Testament, as we have seen, and great national figures as well; but they do not seek adventure in any physical or even heroic sense. The only exception is that of Samson, who is a folk-hero, and even his exploits have been carefully altered or extended in order to endow him with religious qualities which originally he did not in any sense possess.

The reason for this lack of the theme of adventure lies, of course, in the overwhelming religious nature both of writers and of the material with which they deal. Persons in the Old Testament go on quests just as do those in the epics and sagas; but their quests do not arise from the desire for personal glory and honor or from patriotic fervor in itself. They arise instead from the plans and designs of God for His people or as the result of His direct commands. Inevitably this fact accounts for the spiritual atmosphere which surrounds them and which causes them to be seen as imaginative ideas as well as actual journeys.

Abraham journeys with his father from Ur of the Chaldees and its idols to Haran, and thence to the Land of Canaan, in order to find a home where he may live with his God and perpetuate the Hebrew race. On his later sad and bitter journey from Beersheba to Moriah to sacrifice his son Isaac, he is both fulfilling God's awful command and searching for its meaning. When Jacob resolves to leave Padan-aram in Syria and return to Canaan, he is not only traveling from one place to another, but going back to the beginnings of his tribe in his own land. The pillar of cloud which moves above and before the Children of Israel and which determines always whether they are to stay at one place in the wilderness or to move on to another endows their long journey from Egypt toward their Promised Land with added spiritual significance.

This significance extends even to far more brief and less important journeyings in the Old Testament; and in a singular, yet sure way makes them prototypes or originals of thousands of similar journeys taken at all times and by all manner of people. The first chapter of the book of I Samuel recounts a yearly journey taken by a typical village family, that of a man named Elkanah, who lived in Ramah with his two wives, Hannah and Peninnah. They go each year to the temple at Shiloh to offer sacrifice. The preparations for such a pilgrimage we can well imagine, the excitement it meant to parents and children alike. For, although its end was a religious one, it afforded as well along the way quite human and earthly pleasures, meeting and talking with friends and strangers bound for the same goal, seeing new and unfamiliar sights. And the decision of Hannah, once she had obtained from God the promise which she sought, to forego such excursions in the future in order to stay at home with her baby doubtless involved many personal sacrifices, understood by all women who long for a change of scene. This simple story has trailed its common meaning through many centuries just as has the later and more familiar story of Naomi and her daughter-in-law, Ruth, the Moabitess. Naomi's return home to her own country and her own religion after years away from both has been recalled for more than two thousand years by people journeying under like circumstances; and Ruth is always the hopeful, yet bewildered emigrant, traveling to a strange land.

Thus no journey in the Old Testament is ever prompted merely by the spirit of adventure or taken for its own sake. All travelers seek something: Abraham, Rebekah, Jacob, Caleb and Joshua, Obadiah, Elijah and Elisha, Naaman, Jonah, and the frightened woman of Tekoa, to name but a few. They may be looking for lost asses, or an increase in flocks, or corn in Egypt, or a wife, or grass and water, or an inspired prophet, or a new home, or the assurance of acceptance in an old one after a long time away. They may be fulfilling a welcome or even unwelcome command of God. And no journey is ever undertaken around which there is not thrown the presence of God, always as a participant and often even as a fellow-traveler and guide.

This is especially true of the long and hazardous journey taken by the exiles in Babylon on their Return to Jerusalem. It is impossible to overestimate the importance of this journey, this return home after fifty years in an alien land—a journey undertaken not by the original exiles themselves, but determined upon by their children and grandchildren who knew of their homeland only through tales and traditions. To the sensitive imagination this return to Judea and Jerusalem has no parallel even among the earliest wanderings from the desert, or the exodus from Egypt, or the entrance into Canaan. For upon it depended not only the resurrection of the Hebrew state and nation, but quite literally the survival of an ancient civilization and the assurance of its gifts to future ages, the most important of which was, of course, the Old Testament itself.

We have no actual, or at least reliable, record of this eight-hundred-mile journey across the deserts from Babylon to Judea, upon which went not only people, but the Hebraic legacy to the Western world. The figures of the number who took it, given in the books of Ezra and Nehemiah as forty-two thousand persons of various tribes and families, besides some seven thousand servants, can hardly be accurate because of the physical impossibility of transporting such a huge company across barren, inhospitable country. But one likes to think even of a far smaller number, and perhaps even of several companies at different times, moving ever onward, encouraged by their choirs of "singing men and singing women," who accompanied them not only for consolation on the way, but for the observance of the Sabbath and for the celebration of other religious ceremonies.

This momentous journey, although any actual account of it is lacking, is the source and subject of some of the most beautiful of Hebrew poetry, that of Second Isaiah,

who is often known as the Poet of the Exile and some of
whose lines have already been quoted to illustrate the
quality of wonder intrinsic to the Hebrew mind. From
the 40th to the 55th chapters of the book of Isaiah and
perhaps also in other chapters, notably the 35th, he is giving hope and assurance to those who are about to set
forth upon it. Although he speaks, first, as a prophet called
by God both to urge upon His people their return home
and to proclaim His nature as the One and Only God,
besides whom there is no other, he is yet primarily a poet,
distinguished by a freedom and an ecstasy unexcelled in
Hebrew poetry.

He pictures the journey homeward in a series of images
in which "the everyday and the low" are, indeed, raised
to "sublimity." In his imagination the crooked and bewil-
dering paths across the desert become a highway, clear
and straight; weak hands become strong; feeble knees are
given power; barren rocks gush forth with water; the
tangled lairs of wild beasts are transformed into grassy
places; trees with their welcome shade spring up in the
arid wastes, the cedar instead of the thorn, the myrtle instead of the briar; wine and milk abound for all without
price; and darkness is constantly transfused by light. Thus
all physical nature is in league with the spiritual aspirations
of a people. The journey throughout is seen as a quest,
a search, in which human feet, free from lameness, bear the
redeemed soul of man away from exile, home to Jerusalem,
of old the sanctuary of God:

> Thus saith the Lord, thy Redeemer,
> The Holy One of Israel:
> I am the Lord, and there is none else;
> There is no God beside me.
> I form the light and create darkness.
> I the Lord have called thee in righteousness
> And will hold thy hand and will keep thee,
> And give thee for a covenant of the people,
> To open the blind eyes,

To bring out the prisoners from the prison,
And them that sit in darkness out of the prison house.
Go ye forth of Babylon
Flee ye from the Chaldeans,
With a voice of singing declare ye,
Tell this, utter it even to the end of the earth:
Say ye, The Lord hath redeemed his servant Jacob.
Remember ye not the former things,
Neither consider the things of old.
Behold I will do a new thing;
Now it shall spring forth, shall ye not know it?
I will even make a way in the wilderness,
And rivers in the desert.
The beast of the field shall honor me,
The dragons and the owls,
Because I give waters in the wilderness
To give drink to my people, my chosen.

And yet it is an earthly journey which the poet foretells, one to be undertaken as it was in reality undertaken from Babylon to Judea. Several of the Psalmists also base their poems upon earthly journeys although these, too, are seen in terms of the restless human spirit. Such psalms are known as Pilgrim Songs because they were supposedly written to be sung by bands of pilgrims as they approached Jerusalem on the occasion of high religious festivals or holy days. The familiar 121st psalm is such a pilgrim song, sung as the wanderers first see the hills above the Holy City and suggesting in its images of heat and of danger the journey which they have taken across the deserts:

I will lift up mine eyes unto the hills
From whence cometh my help.
My help cometh from the Lord,
Which made heaven and earth.
He will not suffer thy foot to be moved,
He that keepeth thee will not slumber,
Behold, he that keepeth Israel
Shall neither slumber nor sleep.
The Lord is thy keeper,

The Lord is thy shade upon thy right hand.
The sun shall not smite thee by day,
Nor the moon by night.
The Lord shall preserve thee from all evil,
He shall preserve thy soul.
The Lord shall preserve thy going out and thy coming in
From this time forth and even for evermore.

These physical journeyings of the Old Testament, always prophetic of the spiritual, have their spiritual complements or counterparts in those books or in single poems and passages which deal with the journeys of the mind and soul. To *seek*, to *search*, or to *have sought* are terms repeatedly used in Old Testament poetry. The long poem of Job is a search into the problem of pain and suffering in the world, a search after the nature of God. In the light of human experience can He be just toward the children of men?

Oh, that I knew where I might find him!
That I might come even to his seat!
I would order my cause before him,
I would know the words which he would answer me,
And understand what he would say unto me.
Will he plead against me with his great power?
No; but he would put strength in me.
Behold, I go forward, but he is not there,
And backward, but I cannot perceive him.
On the left hand where he doth work,
But I cannot behold him.
He hideth himself on the right hand,
That I cannot see him.

Ecclesiastes, the Preacher, in his similar though less profound quest, finds no proof of that justice, although he has given his heart "to seek and search out by wisdom concerning all things that are done under heaven":

I returned and saw under the sun
That the race is not to the swift,

Nor the battle to the strong,
Neither bread to the wise,
Nor yet riches to men of understanding,
Nor yet favor to men of skill;
But time and chance happeneth to them all.
As thou knowest not what is the way of the spirit,
Nor how the bones do grow in the womb of her that is with
* child,*
Even so thou knowest not the works of God who maketh all.

It is characteristic of all the Psalmists that they seek after God "with the whole heart," call upon Him in the "day of trouble," consider "the days of old and the years of ancient times." Yet they cannot always find Him, and their cries of desolation and despair perhaps equal those of assurance and faith. Still He is always the goal of their "diligent search," the only source of Life, and the end of their spiritual journeyings:

I sought the Lord and he heard me
And delivered me from all my fears.
This poor man cried, and the Lord heard him
And saved him out of all his troubles.
The young lions do lack and suffer hunger,
But they that seek the Lord shall not want any good thing.
The Lord is nigh unto them that are of a broken heart,
And saveth such as be of a contrite spirit.
The Lord redeemeth the soul of his servants,
And none of them that trust in him shall be desolate.

III

Of all the imaginative ideas in the Old Testament, the one which has endured longest in the mind of the Hebrew people, which is as powerful today as in its beginning, is the idea of Jerusalem as the Holy City. This idea is found in the earliest written narratives and is constantly increased in the strength and beauty accorded it by prophets and by poets. Yet its survival for three thousand years, both among its own race and among others, is explained more truly by natural human aspiration and longing than either by its history or by the literature which it has created.

The actual history of Jerusalem seems simple and slight indeed in comparison with the associations which through the centuries have gathered about its name. In 1000 B.C. and perhaps long before, it was the hill stronghold of a Canaanitish tribe called the Jebusites, whose names for it were Jebus, or Jerusalem, or Zion. Its character of an easily and, in fact, naturally fortified place appealed to David in the eighth year of his reign as king of Israel; and he thereupon seized it and made it his capital city. It was henceforth known as the city of David, a name which frequently occurs in the books of Kings and Chronicles; but it is used mostly to designate the burial place of kings and seems in itself without any mystical significance.

It was not, then, as the city of David that Jerusalem early took upon itself holy associations, but rather *as* Jerusalem, the city of peace, or as Mount Zion, the dwelling-place of the Ark of God and the site of the first Temple. When the earlier prophets, two and a half centuries after its establishment, write of the city, it is always to them *Jerusalem*, or *Zion*, or the *daughter of Zion*. They deplore her sins and foretell her utter destruction as a just punishment from God at the hands of her enemies even more often than they prophesy her final redemption and salvation.

To Isaiah and Jeremiah this daughter of Zion, these high places of God, must be made desolate, forsaken, overthrown and devoured by strangers. Their prophecies concerning her inescapable fate echo profound sorrow and distress. The sacred city, they say, has become an harlot; her silver, dross; her wine, mixed with water. She is left as "a lodge in a garden of cucumbers." She that was once the vineyard of God, His well-beloved, has brought forth only wild grapes and must be trodden down and laid waste under His sorrowful anger. From all her streets shall be taken away "the voice of mirth and gladness, the voice of the bridegroom, the voice of the bride." Her own sun must go down while it is yet day, for her people are lost sheep, led astray by strange shepherds upon her own mountains. Death is come up into her windows and is entered into her palaces. Even God, her one hope and saviour, is as a stranger in His own city and "as a wayfaring man that turneth aside to tarry for a night."

Yet mingled with their images of darkness and death, their bitter outcries against her sins, are always prophecies of her ultimate redemption as the City of God. In their minds she cannot die, for she is the dwelling-place of light. Although her people must be led away into captivity and exile, a remnant must and shall return, after their iniquities have been blotted out, "to sing in the height of Zion," the holy mount of God:

And the Lord will create upon every dwelling-place of mount
    Zion
A cloud and smoke by day,
And the shining of a flaming fire by night.
And there shall be a tabernacle
For a shadow in the daytime from the heat,
And for a place of refuge,
And for a covert from storm and from rain.

The later prophets and poets add image after image to describe her glory which God shall surely re-establish. They call upon her to awake and put on her "beautiful garments"; to arise and shine in the new light which has come to her. They promise that her new foundations shall be laid with sapphires, her windows framed of agates, and her gates of carbuncles; that all her waste places shall burst forth into singing. Multitudes of camels shall come to her, bearing gold and incense to show forth the praises of the Holy One of Israel. Violence shall no more be heard in her land, or destruction within her borders; but her walls shall be called Salvation and her gates, Praise.

Nor in this wealth of imagery, of the fanciful and intangible, are the human beings forgotten, those who once lived in Jerusalem and those who shall return to her. The Lord shall take away her "stay and staff," "the mighty man and the man of war, the judge and the prophet, and the prudent and the ancient." Yet the days shall surely come when her people shall no longer be afflicted, for beauty instead of ashes shall be their portion, "the oil of joy for mourning, the garment of praise for the spirit of heaviness." Her old men, even those with staffs in their hands, "shall dream dreams"; her young men "shall see visions"; and she shall be "full of boys and girls playing in her streets":

> The sons also of them that afflicted thee
> Shall come bending unto thee;
> And all they that despised thee
> Shall bow themselves down at the soles of thy feet.
> And they shall call thee the city of the Lord,
> The Zion of the Holy One of Israel.
> Whereas thou hast been forsaken and hated
> So that no man went through thee,
> I will make thee an eternal excellency,
> A joy of many generations.

To prophets and Psalmists alike Jerusalem is a *quiet habitation*, a *city of truth*, the *joy of the whole earth*. Within her are *all the springs of the soul*. Such conceptions were to endure through the centuries. They influenced not only St. John, who on Patmos and homesick for his native hills, saw in his holy city a New Jerusalem; but they formed the thoughts of poets and philosophers during the early and late Middle Ages in many lands and languages. As they lived on, the conceptions widened to include the spirit of man in all its aspirations, social and intellectual as well as purely religious. William Blake's Jerusalem is the symbol of righteousness and justice to be built "in England's green and pleasant land," even among her "dark Satanic mills."

The ancient idea has become that of refuge from confusion, from the earthly and the material, from all that clouds one's thoughts. Jerusalem is the home of the spirit, of all dreams and visions of the human imagination. She is the symbol of the awakened mind of man, itself "a hiding-place from the wind, a covert from the tempest, the shadow of a great rock in a weary land."

PART THREE

Language in the
Old Testament

1
The Original Language

SINCE already in this book I have often referred to characteristic traits of the language of the Old Testament and of its usage, this final chapter may seem at first glance both repetitive and redundant. It is neither. Whereas in the preceding chapters I have presented the more obvious features of the use of language in order to illustrate certain qualities of the Hebrew mind and imagination, or to contrast the literary effectiveness of the ancient Greek and Hebrew writers, here I want to analyze the language itself; to study its usage in the two great periods of time which mark its change and growth; and to familiarize the reader with its salient peculiarities *as* language. For not only are these peculiarities in themselves unique and important, but a knowledge of them is necessary for any real understanding of the Old Testament.

To be familiar with the mere content of any work of

literature is in no sense to understand it. For it is never the subject matter which confers distinction and power upon a work of art, but rather the *manner* in which that *matter* is presented. This manner includes not only the choice of words itself, but style and tone, form and pattern, various and distinctive literary devices, and even an intrinsic and often intangible spiritual quality, which Marcel Proust calls "a quality of vision, a revelation of a private universe." If the Old Testament deserves, as it surely does, its secure place as one of the great monuments or classics of any literature, it does not hold that high position because of its material, but rather because of the manner in which that material is presented.

Even although very few of us can read the Old Testament in its original Hebrew, we should be acquainted with certain special, even singular characteristics of that ancient tongue. Compared with those languages which we know as Western, or Aryan, the Hebrew language possessed limitations which might well have made it a relatively difficult and inflexible medium of literary expression. As we have already seen, it had no clearly defined tenses in our sense of that term. Its vocabulary was small with no compound words and with comparatively few purely descriptive ones. In its most commonly used words there was a prevalence of hard consonants and many heavy guttural sounds, which would suggest a greater power for emphasis than for melody and rhythm in its literary use. The earliest Hebrew writers and, indeed, many of the later employed an extremely simple word order. They rarely subordinated clause to clause, a method characteristic not only of Latin and Greek, but of later Western languages in general and which in itself makes for ease and flexibility of expression. They instead wrote directly in simple, declarative statements which might well have resulted in monotony.

On its positive side, however, their language possessed at least one remarkable quality which made it, especially in their earlier narratives and poetry, an almost perfect medium of expression. It was primarily a language of the senses and the emotions, one which was seemingly made to arouse and to startle. Many, if not most, of its words were direct, concise, concrete, vivid, and vigorous, like those who spoke and wrote them. For a language is a people; and no language reveals this fact more clearly than does the ancient Hebrew. These simple, vivid, homely words resemble the Anglo-Saxon words in our own language with their concreteness, their strength, and their emotional appeal; and this similarity became of immense importance and value to the English translators of the Old Testament. In fact, in itself it accounts for much of the accuracy and of the tone and spirit of the King James Version.

Such an unpromising and in some ways even defective language might well have made possible only the rude beginnings of a national literature. It is amazing that the ancient Hebrew writers could learn to use it as they did until they had adapted it to practically all forms of literary expression. Like the rudimentary monotheism of their earliest times, it seemed a language framed more for ejaculatory expressions, for curses, war cries, and crude stories of valor than for finished narratives, prophecies, and psalms. Nevertheless, like the development of that early, uncertain monotheism into a full understanding of its meaning until it became the very center of their being as a people, the language constantly took upon itself new graces of expression, became increasingly elastic, flexible, and fitted to any subject, ever more submissive to the demands made by those who fashioned it. Nor did its steady progress toward a wider, more melodious usage owe anything to foreign, outside influence until very late in its history and even then in relatively inconsequential borrowings. Within its own literature there were, to be sure, mighty influences, like that of Jeremiah upon the Psalms or like the profound influence of parts of the book of Deuteronomy which was to lend immeasurable gifts to the later prophets and poets of Israel.

When one attempts to answer the teasing question of how the writers of the Old Testament, early and late, bent their language to their will and their desire, made it serve their high purposes, one finds the answer only in those purposes themselves. Aided though they were, of course, by those habits of mind and character indigenous to them, these alone cannot account for their accomplishment. Its primary source lay in their quality of vision, in the spiritual revelation of their private universe. Their language was their one means at hand to express their entire devotion to their God; to reveal His plans and purposes for them from their beginnings as His own people; and to utter, both as individuals and on behalf of a nation, this tenacious, consuming faith in His eternal goodness and omnipotence. The inspiration of that religious faith, its urgency, even compulsion upon these writers of the Old Testament, was, one must conclude, the underlying, imperishable source of their literary genius.

2

The Two Periods in
Old Testament Literature.

ANY discriminating reader, as he progresses from the earlier portions of the Old Testament to the later, that is from the narratives of the Pentateuch and the historical books to the work of the prophets and of the poets, will discern at once, even in his translation, marked differences in the language itself as well as in its use. Nor are these differences clearly evident only because the earlier books are largely in prose, whereas the later, such as many parts of Isaiah and Jeremiah, Amos and Hosea, as well as all the Psalms, the Song of Songs, and most of Job and Ecclesiastes, are in poetry. There is poetry, too, scattered throughout the earlier books, some of the finest Hebrew poetry, exemplified by the ancient oracles of Balaam, the superb ode of Deborah, and the beautiful elegy of David over the bodies of Saul and Jonathan. Yet this ancient poetry is quite dissimilar in character to the poetry of later centuries, just as the prose written in the time of David around 1000 B.C. or that of the narratives of the patriarchs and judges, composed some two or three centuries later, is totally unlike that of the stories of Ruth or of Esther, of Jonah or of Daniel, all of which belong to a far later period. We often use the term *Biblical language*; but, strictly speaking, there is no such over-all description. Instead, there is the language of the earliest narrators and that of the later; there is the language of the earliest poets and those of a far more advanced age.

These changes in language and in its use, these marked differences in literary treatment, suggest that the literature of the Old Testament falls into ages, or periods similar, shall we say, to the familiar periods of English literature: the Elizabethan Age, the Classical Period, the Romantic Movement, the Victorian Age. This is, in the main true, although in a less easily defined way. For changes of all sorts, whether social, economic, or political, were much more slow in taking place in an ancient civilization; and the literature reflecting these changes or even helping to bring them about was equally slow in its evidence of them. In so remote, secluded, and small a country as that embracing the Hebrew nation and among a people so tenacious of their own traditions and ways of thought, such changes would be even less rapid. The thousand years which cover the literature of the Old Testament do show, it is true, many changes; but they were changes by centuries or even by blocks of centuries rather than by lesser spans of years. Moreover, the lines drawn between these periods or ages are not clear and distinct as are those of much later civilizations, both because the changes themselves were more gradual, and because reliable historical information concerning them has not always been attainable.

It is possible, however, to divide the literature of the Old Testament into two periods or ages, which, although they are by no means so distinct as are similar divisions in the history of later literatures, do serve to differentiate not only the types and kinds of writing within each, but more especially the many changes notable in the use of language. The first of these ages is commonly called the Classical Age of Hebrew Literature; the second, perhaps for want of a more exact term, the Romantic Age. These periods are often called also Pre-Exilic and Post-Exilic; and sometimes the Golden Age and the Silver Age of Hebrew Letters. Literature composed between 1000 B.C., or, in certain instances, even earlier, and the years marking the exile in Babylon from 586 to 536 B.C. is known as *classical;* that during and after the exile, as *romantic.* The terms are hardly exact terms nor are the dates exact dates since certain types or pieces of literature show clear traits of both periods. It must always be remembered also that definite or even closely approximate dates for the composition of several books, or portions of books, of the Old Testament are either impossible to ascertain with accuracy or are still subjects of even violent dispute among scholars. Nevertheless, the division is convenient, and, in a large and, perhaps, somewhat arbitrary sense, reasonably dependable.

To the earlier or Classical Age belong the vivid and familiar legends and folklore, the sagas and single narratives of the Pentateuch (except for the 1st chapter of Genesis) and those of Joshua, Judges, I and II Samuel and certain chapters of Kings. To it also belong the war-song of Nahum; the prophecies of Amos, Micah, and Hosea; those of Isaiah generally accorded to him and of Jeremiah, although, like the unknown writer of Deuteronomy, Jeremiah, who rightly belongs in terms of time to this earlier age, foreshadows the later in much of his writing. To the later or Romantic Age belong the vast majority of the Psalms; the Song of Songs; Proverbs; Ecclesiastes; the stories of Nehemiah, Ruth, Jonah, Esther, and Daniel; the poet, or poets, who wrote the chapters from Isaiah 40 onward; and the book of Job, although certain scholars still hold this period of its composition open to question.[4]

And now as we proceed to examine the language used in each of these vast periods, let us constantly keep in mind the fact of their vastness, the realization that they are not, like the compact Ages of Elizabeth or Victoria in English literature, fifty or seventy-five years in extent, but that instead each covers some five centuries. Within such a space of time more marked difference in language and its use will be apparent than in a short, neat space of mere years. The language of Amos and of Isaiah, writing nearly three hundred years after the brilliant chronicler at the court of David and at least a century after the best narrator of the patriarchal tales, will show a flexibility and fluency unknown to them; and yet in many respects it is similar enough to theirs to belong to the same general period. Or, perhaps more truly, it is so totally unlike the language of the Post-Exilic writers as to be quite foreign to their times. Let us, then, not look for *uniformity*, for precisely the same characteristics in the work of these widely separated writers, but rather for similarity, for traits divergent in some respects, yet basically common in others.

---

[4] As is evident, I am omitting certain books from each period: those containing the Law, various chronicles of the kings, and the work of Ezekiel and the later prophets. These are, except for certain passages, admittedly inferior in literary value and will not be used in this study of Old Testament language.

3
Language in the First Period

IN preceding chapters I have already suggested how certain characteristics of the Hebrew mind and imagination are reflected in the manner of expression used by its writers: in their meagre attention to details; in their use of omission; and especially in the extreme directness and simplicity of their language. I want now to consider more fully the language of the earlier period of their literature so that both its usage and its consequent effectiveness may be clear to its readers.

The first and most distinctive feature of the language in the mind and the hands of its writers is always this unique simplicity. Simple concrete nouns, or pronouns, and verbs form the sharp, clear patterns of sentence after sentence in the early narratives. The nouns carry few modifiers, and the verbs are rarely lengthened by any except the most necessary phrases and clauses:

> And Reuben returned unto the pit; and, behold, Joseph was not in the pit; and he rent his clothes.
> And they went, and came into a harlot's house, named Rahab, and lodged there.
>
> And Cain talked with Abel his brother; and it came to pass, when they were in the field, that Cain rose up against Abel his brother, and slew him.

It is as though the writer were getting down to the bare bones of language, as though he neither desired nor needed more than the absolutely necessary words. This simplicity extends also, as is evident in the examples given, to the word order, which is direct and straightforward like an arrow sent swiftly toward its mark.

Often this simplicity and directness are enforced and

heightened by the device of repetition, either of words or of their meaning, a device always characteristic of Hebrew poetry as we shall see later, but used frequently in prose as well:

> Turn in, my lord, turn in to me.

> Bless me, even me also, O my father.

> They were my brethren, even the sons of my mother.

> Thou dost but hate me and lovest me not.

> And she was his only child; beside her he had neither son nor daughter.

When adjectives are used in these early narratives, they are used sparingly and, for the most part, singly. The same is true in the case of adverbs:

> And Esau came from the field, and he was faint.

> And the damsel was very fair to look upon.

> We have a father, an old man, and a child of his old age, a little one.

> Absalom, the son of David, had a fair sister, whose name was Tamar.

> And Agag came unto him delicately.

> And David came to Saul, and stood before him, and he loved him greatly.

The dialogue of these ancient stories is as direct and simple as are the sparse details of the stories themselves. And there is an almost overwhelming amount of dialogue in the Old Testament since it served not only to move events onward, but often to take the place of both description and exposition. Characters are left to reveal themselves largely in their speech since, as we have seen, they are rarely portrayed or explained by their creators or recorders. Their speech also often conveys the drama of a situation or, as we have seen in Jacob's words at Bethel, the atmosphere or spirit of place. This almost constant dialogue in the Old Testament is pared down in its utterances to its absolute essentials:

> And he said unto them, Is he well? And they said, He is well.

> And they called Rebekah and said unto her, Wilt thou go with this man? And she said, I will go.

> And ye shall tell my father of all my glory in Egypt.

> And the woman conceived, and sent and told David, and said, I am with child.

> And Nathan said unto David, Thou art the man.

The words of Amos to Amaziah, the priest of Bethel, share this same directness:

> I was no prophet, neither was I a prophet's son; but I was a herdman and a gatherer of sycomore fruit.

And Isaiah wastes no words when he relates the stupendous conclusion of his vision in the Temple:

> Also I heard the voice of the Lord, saying, Whom shall I send, and who will go for us? Then said I, Here am I; send me.

Early Hebrew poetry, which, except for that contained in the books of prophecy, is found interspersed among the narratives and is in most cases of a much older date than they, is marked by the same simplicity and vigor of expression. Like all poetry it is more flexible than prose, first, because it is called upon to produce stronger emotional effects, and, second, because, in the case of all Hebrew poetry, its form allowed, even required, more rhythm and stress. The poetry of this first vast period possesses, however, many qualities corresponding to those of its prose. Its lines are, for the most part, brief and concise, impelled by the same urgency and strength; it is distinguished by a similar restraint and economy and by a vigor which seems almost crude in comparison with the refined and finished poetry of the second period:

I will sing unto the Lord, for he hath triumphed gloriously!
His horse and his rider hath he thrown into the sea.

Saul hath slain his thousands,
And David his ten thousands.

Gather yourselves together, and hear, ye sons of Jacob,
And hearken unto Israel, your father.

Tell it not in Gath,
Publish it not in the streets of Askelon,
Lest the daughters of the Philistines rejoice,
Lest the daughters of the uncircumcised triumph.

Blessed above women shall Jael the wife of Heber the Kenite
  be!
Blessed shall she be among women in the tent!
He asked water; she gave milk;
She brought forth butter in a lordly dish.
She put her hand to the nail,
And her right hand to the workmen's hammer;
And with the hammer she smote Sisera,
She smote off his head,
When she had pierced and stricken through his temples.
At her feet he bowed, he fell, he lay down;
At her feet he bowed, he fell;
Where he bowed, there he fell down dead.

The early prophets in much of their poetry show the

same usages of language as do these ancient odes, war-
songs, blessings, and elegies. Amos echoes the poets long
before his day when he reviles the people of Israel for
their hypocrisy and for their false and empty oblations:

I hate, I despise your feast days,
And I will not smell in your solemn assemblies.
Though ye offer me burnt offerings, I will not accept them,
Neither will I regard the peace offerings of your fat beasts.
Take away from me the noise of thy songs;
For I will not hear the melody of thy viols.

Micah, the countryman from the tiny village of Moresheth,
who hated and feared the wealth and oppression of cities,
cries out against them in the language and accents of the
earlier poets:

What is the transgression of Jacob? Is it not Samaria?
And what are the high places of Judah? Are they not Jerusalem?
They covet fields, and take them by violence,
And houses, and take them away.

Isaiah, their contemporary, in his biting, terrible words is
not far removed except in mere time from the unknown
poet of the song of Deborah when she upbraided the indifferent tribes for not rallying to her standard:

How is the faithful city become a harlot!
It was full of judgment, righteousness lodged in it,
But now, murderers.
Your country is desolate, your cities are burned with fire,
Your land, strangers devour it in your presence,
And it is desolate, as overthrown by strangers.

And Jeremiah's awful curse might well have been uttered
centuries before his own day:

Cursed be the day wherein I was born!
Let not the day wherein my mother bare me be blessed!

Cursed be the man who brought tidings to my father, saying,
A man child is born unto thee!

It is true that these earliest and greatest prophets of the eighth and seventh centuries B.C. often wrote in longer, more rhythmical lines with far more elaboration, and equally true that in much of their work one can foresee the approach of a new age in literature; and yet so much of the old terseness and vigor, violence, emphasis, and urgency persist in their language that they belong rightly, not only in time but in manner to the early period rather than to the later.

Figures of speech are much less common to the Classical Age than to the Romantic where they abound in great richness and variety; yet they occur frequently in the earlier language and always add their associative power and value. The writers both of prose and poetry tend not only to draw their figures from familiar images and objects, but also to repeat the same comparisons so often that they have become distinctive and peculiar to the age. Their similes and metaphors have their sources within their homes, or from the daily occupations in towns or villages, or from familiar beasts and birds: ovens or cakes of bread; threshing floors or potters and their wheels; the lion, an ever-present danger and always a symbol of strength and power; the eagle, the partridge, the stork, and the swallow.

The tribe of Judah in the ancient Blessing of Jacob is "a lion's whelp." Isaiah and Nahum liken the Assyrian hosts to "the roaring of lions" and the Assyrian land to "the dwelling-place of lions." "What is stronger than a lion?" asks Samson in his riddle. And in Isaiah's prophecy of peace and righteousness "the lion shall eat straw like the ox." Saul and Jonathan "were swifter than eagles; they were stronger than lions." Both Micah and Isaiah describe peace as the time when men "shall beat their swords into ploughshares and their spears into pruning-hooks." David, fleeing from Saul, compares himself to "a partridge in the mountains," to "a dead dog," and to "a flea." Jeremiah mourns that his sinful people do not know the judgment of God as "the stork in the heaven knoweth her appointed times, and as the turtle and the crane and the swallow observe the time of their coming"; and he cries that the Lord will break them and their city "as one breaketh a potter's vessel that cannot be made whole again." Amos declares that the sins of the people of Israel press upon him "as a cart is pressed that is full of sheaves." And Hosea, who often expresses his grief and sadness in figurative language, likens the adulterers of Israel to an oven, to "a cake not turned," and Israel herself to "a backsliding heifer."

Such figures as these, drawn from habitual, commonplace objects in the ordinary course of human events, from the homely, long-established, time-worn ways of a people, serve to sharpen and illuminate the language and to increase its emotional appeal. Direct, basic, simple, they contribute also by their powers of association and suggestion not a little to the strength of both narratives and poetry in this earlier period of Hebrew literature.

This early language seems designed as well for terse, compact phrases also figurative and yet startlingly literal in their effect, since they are usually framed of concrete, forceful words and images. We hardly realize how in the course of a single day we use these vivid Old Testament expressions to record or describe our doings, our moods and feelings, our hopes, our fears, our narrow escapes, the demands made upon us *on our right hand and on our left.* They have become such part and parcel of our common speech that we have forgotten their ancient origin, their creation in the minds of men sensitive not only to every possibility of their language, but also to every emotional heritage of mankind:

We are *hewers of wood and drawers of water;* earn our bread by *the sweat of our faces* and by the *work of our hands; rest from our labors;* and tolerate or welcome *strangers within our gates.* We sit in *sackcloth and ashes;* eat *sour grapes;* discover that like the leopard we cannot *change our spots;* long to be *giants in the earth,* but are satisfied if we can but *quit ourselves like men.* We are *brands plucked from the burning,* escape *by the skin of our teeth,* take our *lives in our hands.* We *pour out our wrath;* worry about our *children and our children's children* lest they *bring down our gray hairs in sorrow to the grave.* And we eventually *return to dust* when, if we are favored, we become *old and full of days.*

These pithy, compressed delineations of the daily affairs of men *from generation to generation,* with their brilliant flashes of understanding, run throughout the early literature of the Old Testament and bring both the behavior and the thoughts of patriarchs, heroes, poets, and prophets into sharp relief. Its language would be infinitely poorer without them. They survive to *increase and multiply* abundantly in *the days and years to come* of the second vast period of Hebrew literature.

As we shall see, this second or Romantic Age of Hebrew letters is in many ways more rich in the products of imagination both because its best writings are in poetry, always a more imaginative medium than prose, and because the language has become more pliable, figurative, and rhythmic in the hands and minds of its writers. Yet in these earlier narratives, poems, and prophecies it is imagination which heightens, clarifies, and illuminates matter and manner alike. Its powers of association and relation, of suggestion and creation, of fusing the past and the present, of endowing the everyday and the ordinary with its significance and meaning lie beneath and within all its deceiving simplicities of expression, all its omissions of detail.

The reader of this earlier prose and poetry must constantly demand more of his own imaginative powers than in his study of the later, whatever its special graces. His imagination must, as we have seen, fill omissions; span

empty spaces; discern through its own penetration and vision what is only seemingly not there. The two haunting,
troubled questions of Sisera's mother can create as sensitive perceptions in the imaginative mind as the many more
exalted and profound questions asked by God of Job.
Isaiah's simple song of God's vineyard is as moving as are
the more ecstatic outpourings of the incomparable poet of
those later chapters of the same book. Amos, in his brief
statement that God *took* him as he followed his sheep, can
re-create the lonely solitude of the Tekoan wilderness and
the thoughts born there under "the seven stars and Orion"
as dramatically as can the poet of Job re-create the solitude
and comfort of the grave to which he longs to go, or as the
Psalmist, the rivers of Babylon with their willows, upon
which the exiles hang their harps. The five ungarnished
words which record Jacob's horror as he awakes on the
morning after his wedding are quite enough.

So, although the earliest Hebrew writers seem to be rein-
ing in their language lest it escape them, controlling it by
every means within their power, holding it in constant
bondage to their will, they were perhaps conscious of no
such arduous labor. They were not writing for future civilizations and races of which they had no faintest dream.
They were instead setting down for their own people the
annals of their history, in the long course of which they
saw always the purposes of their God; or recording tales,
legends, and traditions already deeply rooted and familiar,
revered as further proofs of the presence and care of God
through their remote, yet always remembered past; or
speaking and writing the actual utterances of God, which,
they believed, He had himself revealed to them as His
prophets, set apart for the redemption of His erring people.
Behind and within everything which they wrote lay a
tenacious religious conviction and a consuming religious
faith. They used their language as, in their day, both its
nature and their own demanded or suggested, doubtless
secure in the knowledge that those who might hear or read

it needed no explanations or elaborations of those foreordained events already known to them. That their use of it, even in its earliest period as a written language, revealed a literary art unexcelled at any time by any race was, again, one of the many and mysterious spiritual gifts granted them by their God.

4
Language in the Second Period

THE second or Romantic Age of Hebrew letters contains in the realm of poetry its most superb contribution to the Old Testament. Nothing in the Classical Age, except perhaps the Lament, or Elegy of David, the Song of Deborah, both of very ancient date, and certain passages from Isaiah, notably those in chapters 2, 4, 5, and 11, can equal the long poem of Job, the poetry of Second Isaiah, many of the Psalms, and certain portions of the books of Proverbs, the Song of Songs, and Ecclesiastes.

In the field of narrative, however, this second period is unquestionably surpassed by the first. Except for the inimitable story of Jonah and, to a lesser degree, that of Ruth, the narratives do not, in any sense, measure up to those of the Classical Age. The books of Daniel and Esther, both of very late composition, seem and indeed are, except for the apocalyptic passages in Daniel, undistinguished in their use of language and in their tone and spirit when they are set beside the biographical account of David and his court, the Jacob-Joseph saga, and such remarkably told single stories as those of the sacrifice of Isaac, of Jephthah's daughter, of Gideon, of Elijah, and even of Samson.

Why are these things true? Is it only that for some undiscoverable reason more gifted writers of prose appeared in the earlier age, poets of greater genius in the second? Or are there possible reasons latent in their respective times and in the conditions of life under which they lived and worked in these far separated periods? In the case of the narratives these questions are perhaps not too difficult to answer.

The story of David, the earliest narrative in terms of composition, was written to keep alive in the race the account of the founder of the Hebrew State, even of its small empire; and although its brilliant narrator was too much a realist to minimize the shortcomings and even the sins of his subject, he was, nevertheless, depicting a king who was to remain the ideal ruler in all Hebrew minds and who, whatever his failings, was beloved of God for his loyalty and religious faith. The stories of patriarchs and heroes had their roots deep in the traditions and the religious devotion of an ancient people. They were composed in that devotion in order to preserve those traditions; and they are marked by a racial fervor of a timeless character quite absent from the later narratives. The desire and the necessity alike to preserve annals of inherent and even consummate value to a race may conceivably not only demand distinction of those whose words are to save and maintain such material, but also endow such words with dignity and power.

There is racial fervor, to be sure, perhaps too much for literary distinction, in the stories of Daniel and of Esther; but it is *immediate* rather than seasoned and timeless fervor. Both stories were written during a period of persecution of the Jewish people by their Hellenistic conquerors; and the unknown men who wrote them were propagandists before they were artists. Their aim in each case was an immediate one: in the case of Daniel to give hope and courage to those who were struggling against their overlords, the Syrian kings of Alexander's Empire, with their Hellenistic religious practices and moral standards so abhorrent to the subject Jewish people; in the case of Esther to intensify patriotic and nationalistic fervor at a time, probably much the same time, when the race was threatened with disintegration and even death. Their authors were not, like their far distant predecessors, writing in an age of relative security, but in one of insecurity and peril, of intense nationalism, bitter antagonism, and even consuming hatred. It is, therefore, not difficult to see why their work might lack the ease, objectivity, and strength of those matchless narrators of six and eight centuries earlier, even if they themselves had been so gifted in language and in thought as were the earlier artists. The very fact that they were primarily writing to deliver a message, to stir up the spirit of a desperate people, rather than to tell a story for its own sake, its own meaning and value, stood in the way of their literary achievement, not to stress the added fact that the nature of the message itself was hardly one to inspire unusual distinction of language.

It will at once occur to readers already familiar with the books of Ruth and of Jonah that they also are in a sense the work of propagandists, that they also deliver a message. This is true. The message, however (in each case the same), is one of vastly different nature. To convey the idea that God is no respecter of persons, that those of alien birth and even of alien faith are likewise His children, is a far cry from the fomenting of nationalism and hatred, however desperate the situation which was its cause. Moreover, the men who wrote the compassionate and idyllic story of Ruth and the sharp, comic tale of Jonah were artists first and propagandists only secondly; and the manner of their work was clearly as important to them as was the matter, if not more so, noble as was their idea and thesis.

When one tries to explain in any wholly satisfactory way why the poetry of this later period is superior to that of the earlier, the task becomes far more difficult. The answer probably lies largely in the change and progress within the language itself, its growth and inventiveness over several centuries. Yet we have only the language itself and its more skillful use to account for this growth. We cannot go back into the history of the two centuries following the return of the exiles from Babylon and note this and that event which might have contributed to linguistic innovations and additions. The history of the Jewish people between their return home and the conquest of their subject province by the generals of Alexander's Empire in 332 B.C. is almost completely lost as reliable history so far as definite events are concerned, for we know actually little of what happened in Judea during those two hundred years.[5]

The importance of this lack of knowledge becomes evident when we compare it, shall we say, to the clearly discernible influences which were in large measure responsible for the growth and expansion of the English language during the Elizabethan Age. These influences we know: the recent invention of printing; the spread of the New Learning of the Renaissance and Reformation; the growth of the universities; the awakened spirit of adventure and of exploration to distant lands. These and other influences meant revolutionary and far-reaching changes within the language itself, changes which were surely reflected in the literary greatness of the Age. What lesser influences may have been at work in Judea during the centuries which gave to the Old Testament much of its finest poetry, we have small, if any, means of knowing.

From the literature itself we can, it is true, reconstruct certain conditions of life there, mostly bitter and even hopeless. We know that the return of the exiles resulted in disappointment and despair. They found their Holy City in ruins; their lands occupied by alien and hated races; their race itself tainted, as they thought, by intermarriage with foreigners; famine and drought abroad; and their country but an obscure and remote province of the Persian Empire. That from such conditions great poets arose is perhaps but proof that genius is often nurtured by suffering rather than by prosperity.

[5] I have given in *The Bible and the Common Reader*, Part I, Chapter III, a brief, but fairly comprehensive account of the history of the Hebrew people, which may prove valuable to the reader unfamiliar with it.

In addition to a new richness and fluency of language there is also evident in the poetry of this second period of Hebrew literature new religious conceptions and ideas which account for much of its eloquence and beauty. When Amos about 750 B.C. strove to teach the people of Israel that their God was the God as well of the Ethiopians, of the Syrians, and of their ancient enemies, the Philistines, he was uttering a doctrine revolutionary to his day. Yet two centuries later Second Isaiah is not only making this idea of God the underlying theme of all his work, but is adding to it the revelation of God as the creator of the glories of the cosmic universe as do certain of the Psalmists as well as the poet of Job.

Throughout this poetry of the Romantic Age there is often present also a mysticism absent from, or at least undeveloped in, the earlier poetry, although it is surely latent in Isaiah's "great light," which shone around those "in darkness" and "in the shadow of death," and in many of the passages in Hosea and Jeremiah. This mysticism, however, is always distinctly and peculiarly Hebraic; and readers of the Old Testament will do well to become aware of its nature. To the Hebrew imagination, regardless of its depth and richness, there could be no possibility of man's losing himself in God, an idea characteristic of Greek and Hindu mysticism and to certain aspects of Christian as well. In the Hebraic sense of mysticism man must always remain man and God is eternally God, however lofty may be the flights of the human spirit. Whatever inspirations or, indeed, aspirations fired the great prophets, they were always securely anchored to their earth with all its bitter realities; the God who showed Job His wonders could be reverenced, but never entirely reached; and however far the poet of the 139th psalm may fly in his awe and worship, he is yet a man, whose thoughts, only, of God are precious and who begs that God will examine his quite human heart.

This singular interpretation of mysticism, of man's communion with God, endows Hebrew poetry with an intimate, almost naive and ingenuous spiritual quality not present, it seems to me, in any other, at least in like degree. Behind it lies all the simplicity and directness of the earliest narratives. Abraham could venture to argue with God over the destruction of Sodom and Gomorrah, could actually persuade Him to spare Sodom if but ten righteous men could be found therein, only because he was so sure of God's nearness to him and concern with him. Jacob could wrestle all night with the angel of the Lord and say boldly to him at daybreak, "I will not let thee go except thou bless me." Enoch *walked* with God. It was this sure and certain conviction of God's nearness, never dying in the Hebrew mind, which made possible the intimacy of later Hebrew poetry.

Throughout the Old Testament there are apparent these seemingly paradoxical, even mutually exclusive, qualities of God in His relationship with His people. He is closer than hands or feet, and yet eternally remote; forever near, and yet distant; present, and yet absent; hidden, yet revealed; transcendent, yet immanent. There is also a singular respect for man, sinful yet always redeemable, which God himself acknowledges. One recalls His final words to Job out of the whirlwind:

> *Deck thyself now with majesty and excellency,*
> *And array thyself with glory and beauty.*
> *Cast abroad the rage of thy wrath;*
> *And behold every one that is proud, and abase him.*
> *Look on everyone that is proud, and bring him low,*
> *And tread down the wicked in their place.*
> *Then will I also confess unto thee*
> *That thine own right hand can save thee.*

This peculiarly Hebraic understanding of man's relation to God infuses Hebrew poetry with an affirmative, positive quality, so intense as to identify all human aspirations, all human despair, with the aspiration and desolation of its writers. As the ancient narratives widen our earthly experience by identifying it with the universal inheritance of man, so the poetry, especially of this later period, widens our spiritual apprehension by the same power of identification.

Definite foreign influences upon the language of this second period are difficult to assess. It would seem at first sight that they might well have been considerable, surrounded as were the Jewish people by alien influences, subject to foreign domination, and living in a world far more cosmopolitan and sophisticated than that which produced the literature of the Classical Age. Yet it must always be remembered that they were a people tenacious of their own identity as in their earliest beginnings, aloof and exclusive by nature, antagonistic toward foreign ideas, and always convinced of their own peculiar destiny. There are discernible foreign influences upon the material of Ecclesiastes, the author of which seems to have travelled from home and to have known something of the Epicurean philosophy and perhaps even of the Stoic. The rich Oriental imagery of the Song of Songs, found nowhere else in the Old Testament, would suggest Persian and Egyptian influence as would certain of its words. But although the language of Second Isaiah, of Job, and of the Psalms prove immense expansion and progress, the vocabulary of Job in particular being more rich and various than that of any other book in the Old Testament, it is doubtful if this advance can be attributed to any specific or widespread foreign contribution. It is more reasonable to explain these many innovations, whether in increased vocabulary or in new means of expression, by the influence of time itself, by the new experiences and necessities it had brought during the period of the Exile and the dim, unchronicled centuries following the Return. Memory, suffering, disillusionment, terror engendered by apostasy, violence, tension, despair, and a still tenacious faith—all these must have brought their own gifts to a language in the minds and hands of gifted men.

Both in the prose and the poetry of the Romantic Age these changes and innovations are abundantly present, although there are also present the older methods of narrative and always the same basic and characteristic form of poetry, even with its embellishments and new fluency.[6] Brevity, understatement, and omission still occasionally occur in the prose narratives; but there are much less restraint, much more detail, and many more purely descriptive words. The stories are longer than those of the Classical Age; constructions are more various; subordination of clauses is more common; dialogue, though rarely so effective, is more full and free. The poetry has a felicity and richness unknown to that of the earlier period, an increase in vividness and variety of imagery, a swiftness of movement, new and more profound emotional appeal.

In the sections which follow I shall try to illustrate the most important of these many changes in the language and in its use both in the narratives and in the poetry of this new age.

II

The finest narratives of this second period of Hebrew literature are unquestionably those of Ruth and of Jonah. Both have endured for more than two thousand years as models of the short-story form, one as an idyllic romantic tale, the other as a piece of satiric and ironic comedy.

Ruth, written about 450 B.C., although set in the eleventh century "in the days when the judges ruled," is a gracefully told story, distinguished by its quiet, pastoral atmosphere and by the open, courteous nature of all its characters. Slight in its emotional appeal and in its simple presentation of human psychology, it, nevertheless, is told with ease and charm and is brief enough so that its lack of variety in

---

[6] For an explanation of parallelism in Hebrew poetry, that is, of the form governing it, the reader may well study the article on Hebrew poetry in Hastings' *Dictionary of the Bible*. There is a far more brief account in *The Bible and the Common Reader*, Part I, Chapter IV.

style does not become monotonous. The author's natural and direct prose has much in common with that of the older narratives of the Classical Age; yet his work lacks their strength and vitality.

In this later story far more detail is given, and the language itself is more fluent. Emotions, though never profound, are carefully delineated; dialogue is more full; more space is given both to events and to the portrayal of individual characters. Little is left to our perception or our imagination. There is an undertone of poetic rhythm throughout the prose which would have been impossible to the earlier age, but which here adds charm to a tale romantic and idealized by its very nature.

Perhaps there is no better way to become aware of the differences in the narrative methods of the two periods than to compare two similar situations; one, the departure of Rebekah from Padan-aram with the servant of Abraham, who is taking her to Isaac as his bride; the other, the departure of Naomi with Ruth, her daughter-in-law, from the country of Moab to return to Bethlehem:

> And it came to pass that, when Abraham's servant heard their words, he worshipped the Lord, bowing himself to the earth. And the servant brought forth jewels of silver and jewels of gold, and raiment, and gave them to Rebekah; he gave also to her brother and to her mother precious things. And they did eat and drink, he and the men that were with him, and tarried all night. And they rose up in the morning, and he said, Send me away unto my master.
>
> And her brother and her mother said, Let the damsel abide with us a few days, at the least ten; after that she shall go. And he said unto them, Hinder me not, seeing the Lord hath prospered my way. Send me away that I may go to my master. And they said, We will call the damsel and enquire at her mouth.
>
> And they called Rebekah and said unto her, Wilt thou go with this man? And she said, I will go. And they sent away Rebekah their sister, and her nurse,

and Abraham's servant, and his men. And they blessed Rebekah and said unto her, Thou art our sister. Be thou the mother of thousands of millions, and let thy seed possess the gate of those which hate them.

And Rebekah arose, and her damsels, and they rode upon the camels and followed the man. And the servant took Rebekah and went his way.

Then Naomi arose with her daughters in law that she might return from the country of Moab; for she had heard in the country of Moab how that the Lord had visited his people in giving them bread. Wherefore she went forth out of the place where she was, and her two daughters in law with her; and they went on the way to return unto the land of Judah.

And Naomi said unto her two daughters in law, Go, return each to her mother's house. The Lord deal kindly with you as ye have dealt with the dead and with me. The Lord grant you that ye may find rest, each of you in the house of her husband. Then she kissed them; and they lifted up their voice and wept. And they said unto her, Surely we will return with thee unto thy people.

And Naomi said, Turn again, my daughters. Why will ye go with me? Are there yet any more sons in my womb that they may be your husbands? Turn again, my daughters, Go your way; for I am too old to have an husband. If I should say, I have hope, if I should have an husband also tonight and should also bear sons, would ye tarry for them till they were grown? Would ye stay for them from having husbands? Nay, my daughters; for it grieveth me much for your sakes that the hand of the Lord is gone out against me.

And they lifted up their voice and wept again; and Orpah kissed her mother in law; but Ruth clave unto her. And Naomi said, Behold, thy sister in law is gone back unto her people and unto her gods. Return thou after thy sister in law.

And Ruth said, Intreat me not to leave thee, or to return from following after thee. For whither thou goest, I will go; and where thou lodgest, I will lodge.

Thy people shall be my people, and thy God my
God. Where thou diest, will I die, and there will I
be buried. The Lord do so to me and more also, if
aught but death part thee and me.

When she saw that she was steadfastly minded to
go with her, then she left speaking unto her. So
they two went until they came to Bethlehem.

Jonah is without doubt the most brilliantly told story of
the second period. Brief though it is, its characterization is
sharper than that of Ruth, and the characters themselves,
chiefly those of Jonah and of God, his mocking rival, are
far more complex in their conception and presentation. Its
emotions are more varied and profound, and the attitude
of its author, a master of irony, more realistic. There are
few short stories of any time or in any language which ac-
complish so much within so limited a space. Yet it is neither
by brevity nor by omission, as they were used in the narratives of the Classical Age, that the author achieves his
effects, but rather by his own ironic wit and even daring,
effects particularly evident in the last two chapters of his
story.

Written a century at least and perhaps even two centuries after the book of Ruth, Jonah yet has more in common than has Ruth with the earliest Hebrew narratives,
largely because of its author's objective approach. Unlike
the creator of Ruth, who is never absent from his story,
but almost visible within it, the writer of Jonah is as seemingly detached from his as was the ninth-century composer,
or recorder, of the stories of Jacob. Nevertheless, when one
selects a similar situation from the Jacob-Joseph saga, that
of Joseph thrown into the pit by his brothers, and places it
beside the throwing of Jonah into the sea by the super-
stitious sailors, the differences in language of the two
widely-separated authors are easily apparent:

And Israel said unto Joseph, Do not thy brethren
feed the flock in Shechem? Come, and I will send

thee unto them. And he said to him, Here am I. And he said to him, Go, I pray thee, see whether it be well with thy brethren and well with the flocks, and bring me word again. So he sent him out of the vale of Hebron, and he came to Shechem. And Joseph went after his brethren and found them in Dothan.

And when they saw him afar off, even before he came near unto them, they conspired against him to slay him. And they said one to another, Behold, this dreamer cometh! Come now therefore, and let us slay him, and cast him into some pit, and we will say, Some evil beast hath devoured him. And we shall see what will become of his dreams.

And Reuben heard it, and he delivered Joseph out of their hands, and said, Let us not kill him. And Reuben said unto them, Shed no blood, but cast him into this pit that is in the wilderness and lay no hand upon him.

And it came to pass when Joseph was come unto his brethren that they stript Joseph out of his coat, his coat of many colors that was on him. And they took him, and cast him into a pit; and the pit was empty. There was no water in it.

Now the word of the Lord came unto Jonah the son of Amittai, saying, Arise, go to Nineveh, that great city, and cry against it; for their wickedness is come up before me.

But Jonah rose up to flee unto Tarshish from the presence of the Lord, and went down to Joppa. And he found a ship going to Tarshish, so he paid the fare thereof and went down into it to go with them unto Tarshish from the presence of the Lord. But the Lord sent out a great wind into the sea, and there was a mighty tempest in the sea so that the ship was like to be broken.

Then the mariners were afraid, and cried every man unto his god, and cast forth the wares that were in the ship to lighten it of them. But Jonah was gone down into the sides of the ship, and he lay, and was fast asleep.

So the shipmaster came to him, and said unto him, What meanest thou, O sleeper? Arise, call upon thy

God, if so be that God will think upon us, that we perish not. And they said, every one to his fellow, Come, and let us cast lots that we may know for whose cause this evil is upon us. So they cast lots, and the lot fell upon Jonah.

Then said they unto him, Tell us, we pray thee, for whose cause this evil is upon us, What is thine occupation, and whence comest thou? What is thy country, and of what people art thou? And he said unto them, I am an Hebrew; and I fear the Lord, the God of heaven, which hath made the sea and the dry land.

Then were the men exceedingly afraid, and said unto him, Why hast thou done this? (For the men knew that he had fled from the presence of the Lord because he had told them.) What shall we do unto thee that the sea may be calm unto us? And he said unto them, Take me up and cast me forth into the sea, so shall the sea be calm unto you. For I know that for my sake this great tempest is upon you.

Nevertheless the men rowed hard to bring it to the land, but they could not, for the sea wrought, and was tempestuous against them. Wherefore they cried unto the Lord, and said, We beseech thee, O Lord, we beseech thee, let us not perish for this man's life, and lay not upon us innocent blood; for thou, O Lord, hast done as it pleased thee.

So they took up Jonah and cast him forth into the sea. And the sea ceased from her raging.

III

The basic structure of Hebrew poetry remains the same whichever its period. There are the same balanced lines, the same repetition of meaning, the same rhythmic stress and accent. Yet the lines of the later poetry have become lengthened, the construction more flexible, the repetitions more rich and varied, the rhythm more melodious. These changes are apparent when we compare some lines from the Ode of Deborah, written perhaps as early as 1150 B.C. and inserted long afterward in Judges 5, with a passage from the 8th psalm composed seven or more centuries later:

They fought from heaven;
The stars in their courses fought against Sisera.
The river of Kishon swept them away,
That ancient river, the river Kishon.

When I consider thy heavens, the work of thy fingers,
The moon and the stars which thou hast ordained,
What is man that thou art mindful of him?
And the son of man that thou visitest him?

Many of these gradual changes are apparent also in the poetry of the later years of the Classical Age, in the poetry of the Deuteronomist and of the prophets, particularly in that of Isaiah, Hosea, and Jeremiah. Yet even its finest work lacks the fluency, diversity, and rich imagery of the verse of the Romantic Age.

I have already suggested that behind and within the poetry of this age lay certain wider and deeper conceptions of the nature of God and of man's relation to Him, ideas which undoubtedly lent eloquence to its poetic utterances. There were surely also behind it broader fields of knowledge; a new environment such as Babylon to Second Isaiah; wider contact with other peoples and races—all of which influences might well result in an increased delicacy and aptness of both observation and expression and in a new understanding of the powers of language. In other words, time and place, added experience, a longer memory unquestionably lent their gifts as always to the poet. And, finally, there is always the possibility that the poets of the Romantic Age were more gifted men whatever their time and circumstances, just as the genius of Chaucer, of Milton, and of Shakespeare cannot be explained merely by the character of the centuries in which they happened to live.

The language of this later poetry is marked by many innovations and changes in its structure and style. The old restraints which define Classical poetry have given place to grace, abundance, and variety of expression. In the longer, more varied constructions participles appear; subordination of clauses is frequent; imperatives and questions are constantly used; swift alterations in mood and hence in movement are often apparent, the language rising and falling, quickening and slowing with the shifts of emotion. And always, as I have said, there is an intensity and even intimacy of spiritual appeal, a peculiar ingenuousness and candor, a subjective tone, all of which identify the reader more closely with the poet.

All these additional qualities are evident in the following passages, from Second Isaiah 55, from Proverbs 8, and from Job 3, passages which illustrate this later poetry at its best. In the first of these the poet is giving expectancy, spiritual hope, and trust to his people in Babylon, proclaiming those "new things" of the mind and soul of which he is ever the poet and prophet:

Ho, every one that thirsteth, come ye to the waters!
And he that hath no money, come ye, buy and eat!
Yea, come, buy wine and milk without money and without
      price.
Wherefore do ye spend money for that which is not bread?
And your labor for that which satisfieth not?
Hearken diligently unto me, and eat that which is good,
And let your soul delight itself in fatness.
Seek ye the Lord while he may be found;
Call ye upon him while he is near.
Let the wicked forsake his way,
And the unrighteous man his thoughts,
And let him return unto the Lord, and he will have mercy upon
      him,
And to our God, for he will abundantly pardon.
For my thoughts are not your thoughts,
Neither are your ways my ways, saith the Lord.
For as the heavens are higher than the earth
So are my ways higher than your ways,
And my thoughts than your thoughts.

The poem in Proverbs 8, set like a well of water in the midst of hundreds of arid maxims of the sages, is spoken by

Wisdom to describe her Being even before the creation of
the world:

> *The Lord possessed me in the beginning of his way,*
> *Before his works of old.*
> *I was set up from everlasting, from the beginning,*
> *Or even the earth was.*
> *When there were no depths, I was brought forth;*
> *When there were no fountains abounding with water.*
> *Before the mountains were settled,*
> *Before the hills was I brought forth;*
> *While as yet he had not made the earth, nor the fields,*
> *Nor the highest part of the dust of the world.*
> *When he prepared the heavens, I was there;*
> *When he set a compass upon the face of the depth;*
> *When he established the clouds above;*
> *When he appointed the foundations of the earth.*
> *Then was I by him, as one brought up with him,*
> *And I was daily his delight, rejoicing always before him;*
> *Rejoicing in the habitable part of his earth;*
> *And my delights were with the sons of men.*

In the poem from Job, in which he curses his birth and
longs for death, a change of mood brings about a quick
change of rhythm in the language. The tight, abrupt, bitter words give place after some stanzas to a meditative, even
plaintive tone, melodious and moving:

> *Let the day perish wherein I was born;*
> *And the night in which it was said,*
> *There is a man child conceived.*
> *Let that day be darkness;*
> *Let not God regard it from above;*
> *Neither let the light shine upon it.*
> *Let darkness and the shadow of death stain it;*
> *Let the blackness of the day terrify it.*
> *As for that night, let darkness seize upon it;*
> *Let it not be joined unto the days of the year,*
> *Let it not come into the number of the months.*
> *Why died I not from the womb?*
> *Why did I not give up the ghost*
> *When I came out of the belly?*

For now should I have lain still and been quiet,
I should have slept; then had I been at rest
With kings and counsellors of the earth,
Or with princes that had gold,
Who filled their houses with silver.
There the wicked cease from troubling,
And there the weary be at rest.
There the prisoners rest together.
They hear not the voice of the oppressor.
The small and great are there;
And the servant is free from his master.

The abundant imagery of this later·poetry is one of its most outstanding features whether it exists for itself *as* imagery or occurs in personification or in new and more various similes and metaphors. The old, conventional, repeated Classical imagery here gives place to a wealth of fresh conceptions and observations. The nature of the lion, for example, in Job 4 is shown in many different aspects. Countless other forms of animal life appear, particularly in Job, but also in certain psalms, in Proverbs, and in the Song of Songs: the raven, vulture, ostrich, the stork, the turtle-dove; wild goats, hinds, the wild ass, the conies of the rocks, the foxes that spoil the vines. These excite wonder, not only as the works of God, but also because of their unique habits and ways of which the poets are sharply aware. Even the most minute of them are not forgotten; the moth, which is the symbol of destruction; the worm, which to Job has become his mother and his sister; the spider, whose skillful hands build her house even in kings' palaces and the frailty of whose web is symbolic of those forgetful of God. The stars and constellations, mentioned only occasionally by the poets of the Classical Age, are referred to again and again, sometimes identified, as in Job, as Orion, Arcturus, the Pleiades, sometimes, as in the imagination of the Psalmist, numbered by God and called by Him by their familiar names. Snow, hail, hoarfrost, mist, winds, clouds, rain, the springs in the valley—these are used both for their own beauty and as figures of comparison. Flowers and fruits appear not only "on the earth," but carefully distinguished upon the pages: the lily, the rose, the rose of Sharon, the mallow, the almond blossom, the pomegranate, apple, and fig, cinnamon, aloes, and myrrh. Jewels of all sort shed their brilliance: the topaz, the sapphire, rubies, pearls, onyx, and crystal. Trees of every kind are mentioned not only for their shade in a desert land, but as symbols of the life of man, now "planted by the rivers of water," now felled and broken.

Personification delights these later poets. The morning, the evening, the desert, the little hills rejoice; the trees of the woods also rejoice and those of the field clap their hands. The morning stars sing together; the islands fear and keep silence. The fields of Job are pictured as crying and their furrows as complaining. In the many references to song and singing in Second Isaiah, the mountains burst into song as do the waste places of Jerusalem, the wilderness, the isles, the heavens, the earth, the forest "and every tree therein."

The similes and metaphors used are apt and various; yet except for those in the Song of Songs where they suggest foreign influence and seem overdone and even bizarre, they are usually drawn, like those of the earlier age, from familiar objects and occupations. Their deeper emotional appeal arises from the greater richness in language rather than from their source. A shadow, for example, is not a new image. Isaiah uses it with great effectiveness and beauty in far earlier poetry. Yet in the words of the poet of Job it becomes more memorable because of its added power of spiritual association and identification:

> For we are but of yesterday and know nothing,
> Because our days upon earth are a shadow.

> Man that is born of a woman
> Is of few days and full of trouble.
> He cometh forth like a flower and is cut down;
> He fleeth also as a shadow and continueth not.

Many other figures have their sources in the literature of
the past; yet in that past they are rarely used with the intimacy characteristic of these later poets who again and
again probe into the depths of human experience in their
close, personal comparisons:

> For I will pour water upon him that is thirsty,
> And floods upon the dry ground.
> I will pour my spirit upon thy seed,
> And my blessing upon thine offspring;
> And they shall spring up as among the grass,
> As willows by the water courses.
>
> My days are swifter than a weaver's shuttle
> And are spent without hope.
> They are passed away as the swift ships,
> As the eagle that hasteth to the prey.
>
> For thou hast been a shelter for me
> A strong tower from the enemy.
> I will abide in thy tabernacle forever,
> I will trust in the covert of thy wings.
> As the hart panteth after the water brooks,
> So panteth my soul after thee, O God.

In Job 29 and 30, where Job describes his former peace
and dignity and contrasts both with his present anguish of
mind and body, metaphors are lavishly used. These share
the concreteness of the earlier poetry; but they are endowed with new grace and power:

> Oh that I were as in months past,
> As in the days when God preserved me!
> When his candle shined upon my head,
> When by his light I walked through darkness.
> I put on righteousness, and it clothed me;
> My judgment was as a robe and a diadem.
> I was eyes to the blind, and feet was I to the lame.
> My root was spread out by the waters,
> And the dew lay all night upon my branch.
> Men waited for me as for the rain,

And they opened their mouth wide as for the latter rain.
Did not I weep for him that was in trouble?
Was not my soul grieved for the poor?
When I looked for good, then evil came unto me;
And when I waited for light, there came darkness.
I am a brother to dragons,
And a companion to owls.
My skin is black upon me,
And my bones are burned with heat.
My harp also is turned to mourning,
And my organ into the voice of them that weep.

There is a freedom in this imagery unknown to the earlier age; sharper contrasts both in thought and in language; a new quality of vision; a new revelation of a private universe, yet one inhabited by all. Job's bitter disillusionment with the world of man becomes more human and real when placed against his wonder over the world of God. The contrasting moods of the Psalmists, now of despondency, now of faith, echo the griefs and hopes of the ages. The visions of Second Isaiah can still lead "the blind by a way they knew not."

The many advances evident in the poetry of the Romantic Age do not, however, necessarily imply that it is *all* of a higher quality than that of the Classical. Just as there are readers who find in *Paradise Lost* a grandeur not to be found in Keats or in Shelley, or who will always prefer T. S. Eliot to Dylan Thomas, so there may well be those who find in Amos and Isaiah qualities more rewarding and satisfying than the ecstasies of Second Isaiah, or the outpourings of the Psalmists, or even than the superb utterances of the poet of Job. It is undeniably true that this later Hebrew poetry has few rivals in that of the earlier period; and yet that fact is not to minimize the unexcelled best of the great prophets or to discount the miraculous use of the early language in its first odes, oracles, and elegies. In other words, this study of the poetry of the Romantic Age is written not to *convince*, but only to *acquaint* the reader.

IV

There is one literary device so common to the Old Testament from its earliest narratives to its latest poetry that it should not be overlooked. Moreover, it is so characteristic of the Hebrew people, of their mind, their imagination, even of their history as a race, that its constant use seems not only natural, but inherent and indigenous. This literary device is the question.

Questions occur not only frequently, but continually throughout the early narratives. Reuben, returning to the pit into which his brothers have cast Joseph, cries: *The child is not—and I, whither shall I go?* Tamar echoes his words and accents when she cries in her anguish to her brother Amnon: *And I, whither shall I cause my shame to go?* Leah screams at Rachel: *Is it a small matter that thou hast taken my husband? And wouldest thou take away my son's mandrakes also?* The angry ghost of Samuel reproaches Saul: *Why hast thou disquieted me to bring me up?* Jezebel in terror calls from her window: *Had Zimri peace, who slew his master?* David asks: *Is the child dead?*

In the most ancient Hebrew poetry questions add their haunting note. Sisera's mother is not alone in asking them. In the same ode Deborah questions the tribe of Reuben: *Why abodest thou among the sheepfolds?* David's elegy over Abner is a single question: *Know ye not that there is a prince and a great man fallen this day in Israel?* Balaam's wise ass says to her master: *What have I done unto thee that thou hast smitten me these three times?* And Balaam in his oracles which bless Israel cries: *How shall I curse whom God has not cursed?* In Jotham's fable the trees question, the olive, the fig, and the vine: *Should I leave my fatness and go to be promoted over the trees?* asks the olive.

The great prophets recognized the value of the question both to stir the human mind and to express the depths of sadness. *Will a lion roar in the forest when he hath no prey?* cries Amos. *Shall a trumpet be blown in the city and the people not be afraid?* Micah asks: *What does the Lord re-*

quire of thee?, a question repeated by the Deuteronomist, who gives the same answer. Hosea's broken heart is understood in his questions asked of the people both of Israel and of Judah: *O Ephraim, what shall I do unto thee? O Judah, what shall I do unto thee?* The grief of Isaiah underlies his simple words about God's vineyard: *What could have been done more to my vineyard that I have not done in it?* And no sadness could be more profound than that which echoes in Jeremiah's questions: *Is there no balm in Gilead? Is there no physician there?*

God asks questions both in His own words and through the mouths of His prophets. *Where art thou?* He calls to Adam in the garden. *Who told thee that thou wast naked?* He demands of Cain: *Where is Abel thy brother?* He asks of Abraham: *Wherefore did Sarah laugh?*, and of Elijah at Horeb: *What doest thou here, Elijah?* The sad accents of His voice sound in the prophets who speak for Him: *O my people, what have I done unto thee? Wherein have I wearied thee?* He proclaims His universal fatherhood in questions: *Are ye not as children of the Ethiopians unto me, O children of Israel? Have not I brought up Israel out of the land of Egypt? And the Philistines from Caphtor? And the Syrians from Kir?*

Questions multiply exceedingly in all the later poetry. Second Isaiah asks them in a crescendo of repetition:

To whom then will ye liken God?
Or what likeness will ye compare unto him?
Have ye not known? Have ye not heard?
Hath it not been told you from the beginning?
Have ye not understood from the foundations of the earth?

The Psalmists know their power:

Lord, who shall abide in thy tabernacle?
Who shall dwell in thy holy hill?
How long wilt thou hide thy face from me?
How long wilt thou forget me, O Lord? Forever?

How shall we sing the Lord's song in a strange land?

Ecclesiastes brings home his doubts by means of them:

For who knoweth what is good for man in this life?
All the days of his vain life which he spendeth as a shadow?
For who can tell a man what shall be after him under the sun?

The lover in the Song of Songs uses them to describe his sweetheart:

> *Who is she that looketh forth as the morning?*
> *Fair as the moon, clear as the sun,*
> *And terrible as an army with banners?*

But it is, of course, in the book of Job, in the voice of God out of the whirlwind, that questions most magnificently fulfill their purpose. God's awful questions which fill the incomparable 38th chapter have been prepared for by those of Job himself throughout his long argument with his three friends, questions asked of them, of himself, and of God. All these probing questions, whether human or divine, echo the mystery which enfolds the entire poem, the eternal mystery of man's life and of God's place within it:

Then the Lord answered Job out of the whirlwind and said:
  Who is this that darkeneth counsel by words without
    knowledge?
  Gird up now thy loins like a man,
  For I will demand of thee and answer thou me.
  Where wast thou when I laid the foundations of the earth?
  Declare, if thou hast understanding.
  Who hath laid the measures thereof, if thou knowest?
  Or who hath stretched the line upon it?
  Or who shut up the sea with doors when it brake forth
  As if it had issued out of the womb?
  Hast thou commanded the morning since thy days,
  And caused the dayspring to know his place?
  Have the gates of death been opened unto thee?

Or hast thou seen the doors of the shadow of death?
Where is the way where light dwelleth?
And as for darkness, where is the place thereof?
Knowest thou it because thou wast then born?
Or because the number of thy days is great?

This device of the question throughout the Old Testament is peculiarly Hebraic. One becomes convinced that the Hebrew writers recognized its power, above any other sentence form, of association and identification, qualities which, as we have seen, distinguished their imagination. Their constant questioning creates a pattern or design, frail perhaps, but always visible, which lends a singular unity of effect to the Old Testament as a whole in spite of its diversity. It suggests, too, the long seeking of a people after the mysterious ways of God, apart from which they recognized no life.

This eternal search, in which the genius of both narrators and poets enlist the souls of all men, lies within all Old Testament questions from those of Abraham to those of Job.

v

Readers of the Old Testament should, of course, become early aware that there are vast divergences in the literary quality of its contents. It is the work of many writers, some remarkably gifted as literary artists, others with far less distinction in their use of language. The author of the book of Ruth is a minor story-teller when compared to that of Jonah; and both fail to reach the standard of the writer of the Jacob stories. Ecclesiastes, with all his urbanity and skill with words, falls far short of the poet of Job, even although he is concerned with the same profound question. The many Psalmists were poets of varying excellence, some quite undistinguished; others of good, but minor quality; a few, magnificent.

In this section of the last chapter of my book, it may prove helpful, and perhaps even illuminating, to compare critically two single examples of late Old Testament poetry, both poems of assured literary value, but one far superior to the other both in its range of thought and in its use of language. The two which I have chosen for this critical comparison are the familiar and generally beloved 23rd psalm and the 90th, which is held by many (and I think rightly) to be the finest literary achievement of the entire Psalter.

But before studying these psalms as works of literary art, let us ask ourselves what actually determines the value of any piece of literature. Surely it is not determined by our own firsthand impressions, by whether we *like* a certain work or do *not* like it. Such a personal reaction is but the most rudimentary beginning of what we call criticism: the forming within our minds of honest, intelligent, sensitive, discriminating judgments. These judgments must rest upon and arise from careful, objective thinking. We must not only share, or try to share, the experience, the thinking, the emotions of the writer; we must, in an imaginative, but very real sense, repeat the process of writing his poem, his essay, his novel, until it becomes our own. Then and then only shall we have become aware of his intention, of what he meant, and wanted, and strove to do by every means within his power: by language and its miraculous uses, by discipline, by fancy, by thought, by wisdom. Perhaps much of this discipline, this difficult process of translating into words what is teasing the mind, is not always a wholly conscious process to the writer; but it is nevertheless inevitably in his mind, and his half-consciousness, or even unconsciousness, of it is perhaps what we define as *genius*.

What, then, can we rightly ask of an author, in this case of an ancient poet? What do we expect him to give to us in terms of aesthetic pleasure, that pleasure discoverable in his use of language, its words, their sound, imagery, movement, flow, rhythm? What do we ask of him in terms of thought, of perception, wider understanding, vision? Or do we actually ask him to *give* us nothing, but instead to *draw from us* understandings and perceptions, to startle our emotions and imagination, to sharpen or quicken our intelligence, in short to impress us in such a way that his work is no longer his, but ours.

If this is what we want from him, and I believe that it is, then *we* must have many things to offer *him*. We must be willing and, indeed, able to discover *his* intention and desire, to grasp its unique quality and character, to see clearly, perhaps through comparison with similar poems, the differences which make his own poem more true, more profound, more universal in its appeal. We must be able to perceive how many emotions he is able to arouse in us, the nature of these, at how many points he touches us. Does he appeal only to our physical senses or to our more obvious and shallow thoughts? Or does he awaken within us conceptions and apprehensions which have heretofore been shadowy, or unreal, or seemingly non-existent? Can he, as God did to Job, shake our minds in pieces until all the frail and scattered relics of our intelligence, our imagination, our powers of vision, our sense of language, our half-formed perceptions lie about us to be assessed frankly as to their value and then, perhaps, to be reassembled in some new, and surprising, measure of order and of strength?

Shall we, then, agree that the real value of any work of literature, that for which it in the last analysis exists, lies in its power to irradiate our minds at every possible point, to sharpen our perceptions, to arouse and refine our emotions, to dispel our ignorance, complacency, and prejudice, to lighten our darkness, and, finally, to reveal to us a new world of the imagination and of the spirit?

And now to our two psalms which, for convenience, we must have before us:

The Lord is my shepherd; I shall not want.
He maketh me to lie down in green pastures;
He leadeth me beside the still waters.
He restoreth my soul.
He leadeth me in the paths of righteousness for his name's sake.
Yea, though I walk through the valley of the shadow of death,

I will fear no evil,
For thou art with me;
Thy rod and thy staff, they comfort me.
Thou preparest a table before me in the presence of my enemies;
Thou anointest my head with oil;
My cup runneth over.
Surely goodness and mercy shall follow me all the days of my
*   life,*
And I will dwell in the house of the Lord for ever.

Lord, thou hast been our dwelling place in all generations.
Before the mountains were brought forth,
Or even thou hadst formed the earth and the world,
Even from everlasting to everlasting, thou art God.
Thou turnest man to destruction,
And sayest, Return, ye children of men.
For a thousand years in thy sight are but as yesterday when it is
*   past,*
And as a watch in the night.
Thou carriest them away as with a flood;
They are as a sleep.
In the morning they are like grass which groweth up.
In the morning it flourisheth and groweth up;
In the evening it is cut down, and withereth.
For we are consumed by thine anger,
And by thy wrath are we troubled.
Thou hast set our iniquities before thee,
Our secret sins in the light of thy countenance.
For all our days are passed away in thy wrath;
We spend our years as a tale that is told.
The days of our years are threescore years and ten,
And if by reason of strength they be fourscore years,
Yet is their strength labor and sorrow,
For it is soon cut off, and we fly away.
Who knoweth the power of thine anger?
Even according to thy fear, so is thy wrath.
So teach us to number our days
That we may apply our hearts unto wisdom.
Return, O Lord, how long?
And let it repent thee concerning thy servants.
O satisfy us early with thy mercy
That we may rejoice and be glad all our days.

Make us glad according to the days wherein thou hast afflicted
   us,
And the years wherein we have seen evil.
Let thy work appear unto thy servants,
And thy glory unto their children.
And let the beauty of the Lord our God be upon us.
And establish thou the work of our hands upon us;
Yea, the work of our hands establish thou it.

The 23rd psalm is distinguished, first of all, by the fact that it is without doubt the most widely known single piece of Hebrew literature. There are few people, even among those completely unfamiliar with the Old Testament, who do not know it. They have memorized it in childhood, have heard it read at ninety-nine out of a hundred funerals, and have gathered the mistaken idea that it is the unexcelled poem of a matchless poet. What actually is its value as a work of literary art?

No one of any critical sense will, of course, deny its literary charm or its emotional appeal. But let us ask ourselves candidly what is the source of each? The literary charm and even excellence lie primarily in its language, in its melodious flow of words. All its images are familiar, deeply personal, and full of sensuous appeal: a shepherd and his flock; green pastures and still waters; a table at which one sits in security and safety; the valley of the shadow of death. Having gratefully recognized these qualities, we study its thought and meaning. What does it say that we have not all our lives known? What does its poet demand of us which we cannot easily give him? What is his understanding of the nature of God? How wide and real is the world of human experience which he presents in his beautiful words? Does he, in fact, appeal to anything deeper within us than our desire for safety; our longing to have our fears dispelled; our need for protection? Does he demolish the walls of our small mental and spiritual houses and give us any wider vision of the life of all men from everlasting to everlasting? It is significant that his pronouns are all singular and personal. He never goes beyond the *I* and the *me*.

If these things are not only true but quite obvious once we have taken time to think about them, they can become only more true when we read and study the 90th psalm. The first and simplest contrast between it and the 23rd lies in its pronouns. The *I* and the *me* are non-existent. This poet is writing of all men, in all generations, who are one, "the children of men." He deals with *our* and with *us*. Through his mind and language we are no longer in our narrow houses; they have been shaken down, swept away from any given time or place. We are suddenly shown to ourselves as but a part of a whole, the whole race of men from the beginning until now.

What is God to this poet? Does He lead you and me safely by the hand, or does He instead reveal himself to us as the Creator of the ends of the earth, who is our dwelling-place, only if we can even incompletely grasp His eternal purposes for all men and recognize His mystery? This poet describes all time when he writes of the ceaseless ebb and flow of man's destruction and his return, which symbolize, of course, the slow struggle of the human spirit toward truth and ultimate perfection. He describes, too, the brief span of human life, in which we may nevertheless rejoice and the sorrows and evils of which may arouse our compassion since they are the common lot of man.

What of his language? His images may lack the emotional appeal of those of the 23rd psalm, but they possess surely greater depth and strength. We do not read his poem with our eyes, but with our minds. His language has a dignity, variety, sweep, and power quite absent from that of the 23rd psalm. It is like the sound of an organ as contrasted with that of a flute. Both are undeniably beautiful; yet one solaces, and the other stirs us.

Can there be any question as to which of the two poems is the greater work of art?

VI

The Old Testament is the history of a race, the revelation of its mind, the record of its eternal, restless search after "the things of God." If it were only that, in the hands and minds of gifted men, it would rightly deserve immortality. But it is more. For these ancient men by their wisdom, desire, and compassion, by their understanding of the power of language, and by their imagination which carried them from their bare Judean hills to the uttermost parts of the earth, have transformed a thousand years of human life into the countless centuries of man's experience. It is surely not by chance that the term *every man* occurs numberless times in both Old Testament prose and poetry. For the Old Testament is the record of the life of every man, in every age and place, throughout all the perils and the compensations of his threescore years and ten.

A Bibliographical Conclusion

ALL BOOKS such as this demand a bibliography; and yet I do not know how to give one in its usual sense. Clearly many of my ideas and much of my material must have come from far better minds and books than my own; but it is difficult to discover any exact source for them.

There are books which I have known for many or for several years and which have been of great help to me; there are also articles which I have read with delight and profit. Chief among the books I would name Robert Pfeiffer's indispensable *Introduction to the Old Testament*; Samuel Terrien's *The Psalms and Their Meaning for Today*; R. B. Y. Scott's *The Relevance of the Prophets*; Sir Gilbert Murray's *The Rise of the Greek Epic*; and Eric Auerbach's recent and valuable *Mimesis*, especially its first chapter. For articles, I have found of great interest George Adam Smith's "The Hebrew Genius" in that fine collection, *The Legacy of Israel*, and the truly wonderful recent articles by Edmund Wilson in *The New Yorker*: "On Reading Genesis," "Eretz Yisrael," and "The Scrolls from the Dead Sea."

Much of my book, however, has no definite source which I can honestly name. It is rather the result of a lifetime spent in reading, teaching, and thinking about the Old Testament; and it dates back many years to my childhood when a knowledge of Old Testament stories and the memorizing of countless psalms and of passages from the prophets and the book of Job were a part of my daily existence both at home and in school. I suppose that my mother is the ultimate source of this book. She knew the Old Testament, read it daily all her life with delight, and required its reading and recital of her children.

In more recent years I have spent really thrilling hours in talking about its literature in terms not only of history and sources, but of literary value and charm with people who have contributed immeasurably both to my knowledge and to my enthusiasm. Among these I would name especially Virginia Corwin, Professor of Religion and Biblical Literature at Smith College, whose profound learning I have drawn upon for years and whose interest and kindness have been boundless; Alfred Kazin, William Allan Neilson Professor of English at Smith during 1954–1955, who himself knows the Old Testament and who read my manuscript; Edith Chrystal, sometime Vice-Principal of Newnham College, Cambridge University, and Don of Semitic Languages, who in 1947 and 1948 taught me Hebrew and many less tangible things; Nora Chadwick, Lecturer in Celtic Languages and Literature at Cambridge, who also read my manuscript and thought it worth doing; Robert Pfeiffer of Harvard, who with all his vast learning has respected my own small knowledge and given me always encouragement in my teaching and writing; and the late Professor E. L. Sukenik, of the Hebrew University in Jerusalem, who could fire a stone with interest over the first of the Dead Sea Scrolls, particularly the Isaiah.

Of course there are many other books and people who have been of great help to me, particularly hundreds, even thousands of Smith students who have studied the Old Testament with me over twenty years and whom I can never thank sufficiently for their eagerness, even for their forbearance. The Old Testament to most of them when we began our study was an unopened book. That many of them found in it enduring satisfaction and pleasure has given me my own chief satisfaction and pleasure throughout many years at Smith College.

If those who are now reading these closing words have gained from this book even a small fraction of the complete enjoyment I have had in writing it, all the days and months and years which have gone into that writing will have been worth everything to me.